Communications
in Computer and Information Science   **1295**

More information about this series at http://www.springer.com/series/7899

Juan I. Godino-Llorente (Ed.)

Automatic Assessment of Parkinsonian Speech

First Workshop, AAPS 2019
Cambridge, Massachussets, USA, September 20–21, 2019
Revised Selected Papers

 Springer

Editor
Juan I. Godino-Llorente 🆔
Universidad Politécnica de Madrid
Madrid, Spain

ISSN 1865-0929   ISSN 1865-0937 (electronic)
Communications in Computer and Information Science
ISBN 978-3-030-65653-9   ISBN 978-3-030-65654-6 (eBook)
https://doi.org/10.1007/978-3-030-65654-6

This Springer imprint is published by the registered company Springer Nature Switzerland AG
The registered company address is: Gewerbestrasse 11, 6330 Cham, Switzerland

Preface

Parkinson's disease affects the cells producing dopamine in the brain. Symptoms include muscle rigidity, tremors, and changes in the speech. After diagnosis, treatments can help relieve symptoms, but there is no cure. Thus, an early diagnosis is essential, and the speech is one of those biomarkers requiring more research to evaluate its potentiality for this purpose.

Despite the amount of research in the field, there is still room for developing new knowledge, not only about the characteristics of the speech of people affected with Parkinson's disease, but also about its correlation with the extent of the disease. Automatic systems to evaluate and assess the disease will take advantage of the new knowledge generated in the field to make more accurate and robust systems.

In this context, the aim of the First Automatic Assessment of Parkinsonian Speech (AAPS 2019) workshop was to put together professionals with different backgrounds to discuss and advance in the field of the automatic assessment of parkinsonian speech, fostering interdisciplinary collaboration and interactions. The long term goal is to gain new multi and interdisciplinary knowledge about the interaction among speech and Parkinson's disease, which could be used for diagnosis, assessment, and rehabilitation purposes, especially in the early stages.

During two intense days, in Cambridge, MA, USA, at the headquarters of the Research Laboratory of Electronics (RLE) of the Massachusetts Institute of technology (MIT), AAPS 2019 put together international experts from the fields of machine learning, speech technology, phonetics, neurology, and speech therapy. The long and fruitful discussions during the workshop have led to this book, which collects the most significant contributions to the event. These contributions were selected after a careful peer review of extended versions submitted by the authors who contributed to the event. The event attracted 13 papers in a single track oral session and 3 more poster contributions. After a thorough peer review assisted by the Program Committee, and a lively discussion phase, the Steering Committee decided to accept 6 full papers to be included in the book of post-conference proceedings. These manuscripts are expected to summarize some of the main aspects discussed during the workshop.

We are grateful to the Program and Organizing Committee members, to the reviewers for their invaluable time and effort, and to Springer for their professional support during the production phase of these proceedings. We are also thankful to the participants of the conference and to all authors who submitted their papers for evaluation. Their interest in the AAPS 2019 workshop and their contributions are strongly appreciated.

September 2020   Juan I. Godino-Llorente

Organization

General Chairs

Stefanie Shattuck-Hufnagel   Massachusetts Institute of Technology, USA
Juan I. Godino-Llorente   Universidad Politécnica de Madrid, Spain

Scientific Secretariat

Jeung-Yoon Choi   Massachusetts Institute of Technology, USA
Laureano Moro-Velázquez   Johns Hopkins University, USA

Steering Committee

Najim Dehak   Johns Hopkins University, USA
Juan I. Godino-Llorente   Universidad Politécnica de Madrid, Spain
Mark Hasegawa-Johnson   University of Illinois, USA
Stefanie Shattuck-Hufnagel   Massachusetts Institute of Technology, USA

Program Committee

Alberto Abad   INESC-ID, Portugal
Julián D. Arias-Londoño   Universidad de Antioquia, Colombia
Jose L. Blanco-Murillo   Universidad Politécnica de Madrid, Spain
Germán Castellanos-Domínguez   Universidad Nacional de Colombia, Colombia
Jeung-Yoon Choi   Massachusetts Institute of Technology, USA
Najim Dehak   Johns Hopkins University, USA
José M. Díaz-López   Universidad Politécnica de Madrid, Spain
Juan I. Godino-Llorente   Universidad Politécnica de Madrid, Spain
Jorge A. Gomez-Garcia   Universidad Politécnica de Madrid, Spain
Mark Hasegawa-Johnson   University of Illinois, USA
Max Little   University of Birmingham, UK
Jiri Mekyska   Brno University of Technology, Czech Republic
Laureano Moro-Velazquez   Johns Hopkins University, USA
Rafael Orozco-Arroyave   Universidad de Antioquia, Colombia
José L. Rodríguez-Vázquez   Universidad Politécnica de Madrid, Spain
Jan Rusz   Czech Technical University, Czech Republic
Stefanie Shattuck-Hufnagel   Massachusetts Institute of Technology, USA
Athanasios Tsanas   The University of Edinburgh, UK
Matías Zañartu   Universidad Técnica Federico Santa María, Chile

Local Organizing Committee

José M. Díaz-López   Universidad Politécnica de Madrid, Spain
Jorge A. Gómez-García   Universidad Politécnica de Madrid, Spain
José Peinado Serrano   Universidad Politécnica de Madrid, Spain
José L. Rodríguez-Vázquez   Universidad Politécnica de Madrid, Spain

Sponsors

MISTI Global Seed Funds Award
Massachusetts Institute of Technology, USA
Universidad Politécnica de Madrid, Spain

MIT International Science &
Technology Initiatives

Massachusetts
Institute of
Technology

This activity is framed in the MISTI project "Objective Evaluation of Parkinson's Disease and other parkinsonisms from the speech" funded by MISTI Global Seed Funds Award, and being developed by the Massachusetts Institute of Technology, USA, and the Universidad Politécnica de Madrid, Spain.

Contents

Acoustic Analysis and Voice Quality in Parkinson Disease   1
   Jody Kreiman and Bruce R. Gerratt

Sources of Intraspeaker Variation in Parkinsonian Speech Related
to Speaking Style   24
   Jason A. Whitfield

A Review of the Use of Prosodic Aspects of Speech for the Automatic
Detection and Assessment of Parkinson's Disease   42
   Laureano Moro-Velazquez and Najim Dehak

Automatic Processing of Aerodynamic Parameters in Parkinsonian
Dysarthria   60
   Clara Ponchard, Alain Ghio, Lise Crevier Buchman,
   and Didier Demolin

Approaches to Evaluate Parkinsonian Speech Using Artificial Models   77
   J. I. Godino-Llorente, L. Moro-Velázquez, J. A. Gómez-García,
   Jeung-Yoon Choi, N. Dehak, and S. Shattuck-Hufnagel

Predicting UPDRS Scores in Parkinson's Disease Using Voice Signals:
A Deep Learning/Transfer-Learning-Based Approach. 100
   Julián D. Arias-Londoño and Jorge A. Gómez-García

Author Index 125

Acoustic Analysis and Voice Quality in Parkinson Disease

Jody Kreiman[1,2]([✉]) [iD] and Bruce R. Gerratt[1] [iD]

[1] Department of Head and Neck Surgery, UCLA School of Medicine,
Los Angeles, CA, USA
{jkreiman, bgerratt}@ucla.edu
[2] Department of Linguistics, UCLA, Los Angeles, CA, USA

Abstract. Investigators and clinicians have long sought to apply acoustic analysis to track changes in voice quality in Parkinson disease (PD), in order to evaluate or document treatment effects, track disease progression, or to attempt remote automatic diagnosis. These studies have often had disappointing results, so that the best way to apply acoustics to Parkinsonian voice remains an open question. In this paper we argue that past approaches have not lived up to expectations due to a lack of theory relating voice quality to either acoustics or to the physiological changes associated with disease progression. We review the history of acoustic analysis in PD and describe the motivations that have been presented for each measure. We then describe a psychoacoustic model of voice quality, and explore how this model could be applied to develop a comprehensive model of voice in PD. Such a model would explain how acoustics, quality, and voice production interrelate. Without such an understanding, we contend, the goal of meaningful evaluation of voice in PD will remain unachieved.

Keywords: Acoustic assessment of Parkinson disease · Psychoacoustic modeling · Review

Acronyms

APQ:	Amplitude perturbation quotient
APQn:	APQ over n pitch periods
AVQI:	Acoustic voice quality index
CoV:	Coefficient of variation
CPP:	Cepstral peak prominence
D2:	Correlation dimension
DDA:	Average difference of differences between periods in amplitude
DDK:	Diadochokinesis
DDP:	Average difference of differences between periods in frequency
DFA:	Detrended fluctuation analysis
EMD-ER:	Empirical mode decomposition excitation ratio
F0:	Fundamental frequency
F1, F2, F3:	First, second and third formants
GNE:	Glottal-to-noise excitation ratio
HNR:	Harmonics-to-noise ratio

© Springer Nature Switzerland AG 2020
J. I. Godino-Llorente (Ed.): AAPS 2019, CCIS 1295, pp. 1–23, 2020.
https://doi.org/10.1007/978-3-030-65654-6_1

LSVT: Lee Silverman Voice Therapy
LTAS: Long-term average spectrum
MFCC: Mel frequency cepstral coefficient
MFT: Maximum phonation time
MDVP: Multidimensional voice program
NHR: Noise-to-harmonics ratio
PLP: Perceptual linear prediction
PPE: Pitch period entropy
PPQ: Pitch perturbation quotient
PPQn: PPQ over n pitch periods
RAP: Relative average perturbation
RPDE: Recurrent period density entropy
SD: Standard deviation
SPI: Soft phonation index
SPL: Sound pressure level
S/Z: S/Z ratio
VOT: Voice onset time
VSA: Vowel space area
VTI: Voice turbulence index

1 Introduction

It is not hard to understand the ongoing interest in acoustic measurement of voice in Parkinson disease, which seems at first glance to be an obvious choice for patient assessment. Changes in voice quality and speech (possibly reflecting difficulty coordinating articulation, respiration, and phonation) are among the earliest disease symptoms, and may appear long before other motor systems begin to show effects of dopamine depletion [1]. This fact, combined with rapid technical improvements in acoustic analysis over the last decades, has made acoustic analysis an attractive tool for clinical assessment, for evaluation of treatment efficacy, for remote monitoring of disease progression, and for early diagnosis. Such assessment can take place when clinical examination is problematic (for example, if patients find it difficult to travel to a clinic), and therefore may be preferable to perceptual assessment of voice, which can be imprecise, idiosyncratic, and unreliable.

In the face of these attractions, it is easy to overlook the fact that acoustic measurements in and of themselves have no inherent meaning in the absence of a causal relationship to voice production and/or perception [2]. In the context of clinical assessment, we do not measure sound to find out about sound per se; rather, the point is to learn something about the system that produced the sounds. For acoustic voice measurements to be indexical of diagnosis, disease progression, or treatment effects, there must be a meaningful relationship between physiology (the cause) and the acoustic signal (the effect). To the best of our knowledge, however, the relationship between voice production and acoustics in Parkinson disease has never been made explicit, although studying acoustics requires the assumption that such a relationship exists. The first question asked in this paper is thus, What model(s), explicit or assumed, underlie acoustic measurement practices in studies of Parkinson disease?

To address this question, we undertook a thorough review of the literature on acoustic analysis of voice in Parkinson disease. This review focused on establishing what measures researchers have used and the mechanisms that have been proposed or assumed to justify these choices. This review and the significant problems it raises are described in Sect. 2 of this paper. In Sect. 3, we propose a different approach to assessment of voice quality in Parkinson disease that may alleviate some of the issues described.

2 Review of the Literature

2.1 Method

Unlike systematic reviews (e.g., [3]) or meta-analyses (e.g., [4]), which require carefully matched studies, the goal of this literature review was to survey research practices and motivations as broadly as possible. For this reason, our criteria for including a paper were much less formal than those used in focused reviews. Papers were identified by searching PubMed and Google Scholar for "Parkinson disease" combined with additional keywords like "acoustic analysis," "clinical evaluation," and "assessment." Studies returned by these searches were scanned to ensure that they included patients with Parkinson disease and used acoustic measurements to evaluate something about the disease. Papers were additionally screened for any discussion relating choice of measures to physiology or voice quality. We also scanned reference lists from all papers, in an effort to be as comprehensive as possible. Our goal was to be thorough in our review, but not necessarily exhaustive. Finally, papers had to be in English, in peer-reviewed journals, and available online or through the University of California library system. The final set of 106 papers included experimental and descriptive studies, reviews, and case studies (Table 1; for a complete list see the Appendix to this chapter (Table 4)). All studies were carefully reviewed by the first author, who noted the acoustic measures examined, any justification the authors provided for their choice of measures, and any mechanism relating measures to physiology or perception. These details are included in the Appendix.

2.2 Results

Measurements Used to Quantify Voice in Parkinson Disease
Despite early classic papers by Canter [5, 6], who used hand measurements from an oscillograph and a graphic level recorder, research on the acoustic characteristics of Parkinson disease did not really get underway until the mid-1990s (Table 1), corresponding to the increasing availability and sophistication of commercial voice analysis systems like CSpeech [7] and Computer Speech Lab (CSL; Kay-Pentax, Montvale, NJ). Most papers using acoustic analysis to examine Parkinson disease fall into one of two categories. In the first category (columns 1A and 1B in Table 1; n = 51), measures

Table 1. Types of study using acoustic measures in the assessment of Parkinson disease. 1A: Studies comparing patients to a control group using traditional statistical approaches. 1B: Studies comparing patients to a control group using computational approaches. 2: Studies of treatment efficacy. 3: Reviews and meta-analyses. 4: Case studies and methodological reports.

Decade	Study type					
	1A	1B	2	3	4	Total
1961–1970	2					2
1971–1980						0
1981–1990	3			1	1	5
1991–2000	8		5		1	14
2001–2010	10	1	17	6	2	36
2011–2019	13	14	16	4	2	49
Totals	36	15	38	11	6	106

were used to distinguish patients from controls (usually age- and sex-matched speakers without Parkinson disease, but occasionally groups with other neurological disorders), with the goal either of characterizing the voice disorder associated with Parkinson disease (e.g., [5, 8]) or in attempts at instrumental disease diagnosis (e.g., [9]). These 51 papers fall into 2 subgroups: those using traditional statistical approaches to assess group differences (subgroup 1A; n = 36), and those using machine classification techniques (subgroup 1B; n = 15). Although machine classification studies began to appear relatively recently, note that they did not supplant more traditional statistical approaches, which remain common in the current literature (e.g., [10]).

The second major category includes studies describing use of acoustic measures to examine the effects of treatment (e.g., voice or respiratory therapy, including LSVT (e.g., [11]), pallidotomy, levodopa treatment, and deep brain stimulation) on voice (n = 38). All of the reviewed studies in this category used traditional statistical analyses to examine acoustic differences in voice pre- versus post-treatment. Finally, we included reviews and meta-analyses (Group 3; n = 11), case studies, and a methodological report (Group 4; n = 5 and 1, respectively). These studies were reviewed primarily for any discussion of mechanisms or reasons for using particular measures.

Table 2 shows the acoustic measures used to characterize voice in experimental studies (categories 1 and 2; n = 89). Many variants exist for some kinds of physical measure; for example, Buder [12] lists 29 different measures of short-term variation in F0 (usually called jitter). For simplicity, such closely-related measures are grouped together in families in the table. Measures of F0 reflect the perceived pitch of the voice sample. SPL is the primary correlate of perceived loudness. Jitter and shimmer represent short-term variability in the frequency and amplitude of individual cycles of the acoustic waveform; noise measures quantify the relative amounts of periodic and aperiodic energy in the voice signal; and spectral measures reflect the properties of the voice source. Articulatory measures, measures of rate and duration, and tremor measures describe the dynamic features of speech, rather than voice per se, but are included because they also appear in studies of voice. Nonlinear dynamic measures assess irregular or chaotic patterns of vibration that cannot be quantified by linear measures (for example, due to difficulties in tracking F0 accurately). Finally, a variety of measures appear in computational studies (Group 1B). Most of these are not related in any obvious (or even subtle) way to either voice production or perception, but they have proved useful at efficiently characterizing the overall acoustic signal with minimum loss of information.

Measures of F0 are the most commonly used in experimental approaches, appearing in 63/89 studies (70.8%). Measures of jitter (48/89 papers, 53.9%), shimmer (48/89 papers, 53.9%), noise (47/89 papers, 52.8%), and SPL or intensity (34/89 papers, 38.2%) were also widely applied, often in the same papers. Because they appear commonly and in the same studies, these measures (F0, jitter, shimmer, noise, and SPL) will be referred to as the "usual suspects." Additional measures include speaking rate and utterance duration (30/89 papers, 33.7%), aspects of articulation (16/89 papers, 18.0%), nonlinear dynamic measures (13/89 papers, 14.6%) and spectral measures (5/89 papers, 5.6%). This pattern has remained remarkably stable over time: Apart from the advent of a few newer measures like cepstral peak prominence [13] and nonlinear dynamic measures (e.g., [14]), the parameters used to assess voice in Parkinson disease have remained virtually unchanged since at least the late 1980s.

Authors also tend to rely on the same measures across study types, and across treatments when treatments are being compared. Among non-computational studies comparing individuals with Parkinson disease to control groups (study type 1A), 33/36 papers used the usual suspects, with (22 papers) or without (11 papers) 1 or 2 additional measures (LTAS, formant frequencies, phonation time, S/Z, airflow, speaking rate, etc.; cf. [132]), while only 3 papers used completely different measures (tremor characteristics, measures from nonlinear dynamics, formant frequencies). All studies assessing treatment effects measured the usual suspects, with (n = 23) or without (n = 15) other measures (e.g., spectral shape, duration/rate, subharmonics, pitch breaks). Finally, although machine classification studies typically used very large sets of measures ("307 total measures" [17]; "18 sets of measures" [9]), most (10/15) also included the usual suspects.

In summary, of the experimental studies reviewed, 84.3% included measures of F0, SPL, jitter, shimmer, and/or noise. The choice of measures has not varied much with the purpose of the study, and even the machine classification studies reviewed here often relied at least in part on this same set of variables. This dependence on the "usual suspects" has remained constant from the beginnings of acoustic analysis of Parkinsonian voice, and remains in force today.

Which Physical Mechanisms Underlie these Acoustic Choices?

In general, authors do not explain their choice of acoustic measures, or they appeal to tradition and precedent as justification (see Appendix for details). However, two classes of explanation can be inferred from the literature. In the first, voice symptoms hypothetically derive from failures of speech respiratory control:

Bradykinesia of the respiratory mechanism →
    Diminished airflow →
        Decreased loudness, monopitch, monointensity

Table 2. Acoustic measures occurring across the experimental studies. Numbers in column 3 refer to the order of references in the Appendix. See e.g. [15] or [16] for definitions of the various measures.

Measurement family	Includes	Studies
F0	Mean, median, minimum, maximum, range, SD, CoV, # unvoiced frames, # voice breaks, voice break time	1, 3, 5, 7, 11–13, 19, 21, 22, 24, 26, 28, 32–34, 37–41, 43, 44, 47–50, 52–56, 58, 60–66, 71, 73, 77, 78, 80, 81, 83, 85–87, 89–95, 101–106
SPL/Intensity	Mean, range, SD, amplitude CoV, intensity decay, energy, SPI	1, 5, 12, 13, 19, 22, 24, 32–34, 37, 41, 45, 47, 49, 55, 58, 63, 66, 72, 73, 75, 76, 78, 83–86, 91, 93, 100, 102–104
Jitter	Absolute, %, dB, RAP, PPQ, PPQ5, DDP, # subharmonic segments	1, 3, 6, 7, 11, 18, 19, 21, 22, 25, 26, 32, 40, 43, 44, 47–49, 52–54, 58–62, 64–66, 70, 71, 77–81, 87, 89, 90, 92, 94–96, 99, 101, 102, 104, 106
Shimmer	Absolute, %, dB, APQ, APQ3, APQ5, APQ11, APZ, DDA	1, 3, 6, 7, 11, 18, 19, 21, 22, 25, 32, 40, 43, 44, 47–49, 52–54, 58–62, 64–66, 70, 71, 77–81, 87, 89, 90, 92, 94–96, 99, 101, 102, 104, 106
Noise measures	NHR, HNR, CPP, CPP SD, "peak performance ratio," cepstral/spectral index of dysphonia, GNE, vocal fold excitation ratio, VTI	1–3, 6, 11, 18, 19, 21, 22, 25, 26, 32, 40, 43, 47, 48, 52–54, 58–62, 64–66, 71, 77–79, 81, 87–90, 92, 94–96, 99, 101–104, 106
Spectral measures	Low/high spectral ratio, spectral slope, trendline, tilt, LTAS, glottis quotient, speed quotient	2, 3, 18, 22, 48
Other traditional acoustic measures	AVQI, MDVP protocol	18
Articulatory measures	F1, F2, F2 transitions, VSA, VOT, VOT variation, VOT SD, S/Z, spirantization	6, 7, 14, 21, 28, 29, 32, 39, 49, 55, 78, 83, 91, 92, 102, 105
Rate and duration	Maximum phonation time, duration, # pulses/periods, vowel duration, mean phrase rate, syllable duration, syllable rate, syllable rate variation, DDK, pause length, # pauses, vowel fraction	5, 7, 11–14, 19, 21, 26, 28, 32, 34, 38, 39, 41, 45, 49, 55, 56, 63, 64, 76, 78, 83, 85, 86, 91–93, 102, 103
Vocal tremor	Modulation amplitude, modulation frequency, modulation energy ratio, tremor index	15, 19, 21, 24, 33, 77, 80, 94, 95, 102
Nonlinear dynamic measures	RPDE, DFA, PPE, D2, spread1, spread2, EMD-ER	3, 25, 43, 54, 58, 59, 70, 79, 87, 96, 99, 101, 104
Other measures from computational studies	MFCCs, PLP coefficients, relative spectral PLP, wavelet decomposition measures, large panels of similar measures, autocorrelation measures	3, 8–11, 20, 67, 97, 98

(n = 2; e.g., [18, 19]). Measures applied in these studies include F0, SPL, phonation time, S/Z, and diadochokinesis, whose relationship to respiratory function is complicated or in some cases difficult to determine. This model gained little traction in the literature and died out quite quickly.

Many more studies seem to assume the second kind of model, which states that the problem with voice in Parkinson disease originates in the larynx. Three sub-types of this model have appeared: 1) Voice symptoms derive from rigidity of the laryngeal muscles; 2) The problem is hypokinesia; and 3) The problem is poor kinesthetic feedback, leading to the wrong gain in motor control. Reasoning for these models is as follows. In subtype 1:

Increased vocal fold stiffness →
  Lower amplitude vibration, incomplete glottal closure →
    (a) Reduced loudness, increased F0 and breathiness;
    (b) Roughness; and/or
    (c) Monopitch, increased jitter/shimmer

(e.g., [1, 20–22]). These studies typically use usual suspect measures to characterize irregular phonation. This seems reasonable at first glance, but a number of issues arise on further examination. First, there does not appear to be any statistical relationship between F0 or phonatory instability and rigidity scores as measured via the UPDRS (e.g., [23]), so the assumed link between voice production and acoustics may be invalid. Further, treatment with levodopa reduces rigidity, but it has been repeatedly demonstrated that this treatment does not consistently improve laryngeal or articulatory function (e.g., [24, 25]), as this model would seem to predict. We conclude that rigidity of the laryngeal muscles is unlikely to cause Parkinsonian dysphonia.

The second explanation of the relationship between laryngeal findings and Parkinsonian dysphonia states that the problem is hypokinesia, not rigidity:

Inability to tense the vocal folds →
  (a) Subharmonics, voice breaks, noise
  (b) Glottal gap →
      Increased airflow→
        Breathiness
  (c) Irregular or reduced or asymmetrical vibration →
      Hoarseness

(e.g., [26, 27]). As with models positing rigidity as the cause of dysphonia, acoustic measures in these studies include the usual suspects, but especially jitter, shimmer, and noise measures (e.g., [28, 29]), and measures from nonlinear dynamics (e.g., [30, 31]). Also like models associating dysphonia with rigidity, studies have not demonstrated consistent correlations between acoustic and physiological measures. Because investigators make acoustical measurements on the assumption that the measures will tell us something about a patient's status, this general failure to find reliable associations between acoustic and physiological measurements undermines the whole argument.

Model subtype 3 appears in studies of the LSVT approach to treatment of Parkinsonian dysphonia (e.g., [11]). In this model, dysphonia is largely the result of poor kinesthetic feedback:

Inadequate muscle activation, poor kinesthetic feedback →
Wrong gain in motor control →
Rigidity, bradykinesia, hypokinesia, tremor →
Soft voice, monotone, breathiness, hoarseness.

Because LSVT exclusively targets loudness, nearly all studies evaluating the efficacy of this treatment restrict acoustic analysis to measurement of SPL and occasionally F0 (e.g., [4, 32, 33]; see [34], for an exception, and [35] for review). Such studies always focus on the efficacy of treatment variants (study type 2 in Table 1). Because to our knowledge this model has not been evaluated out of the context of treatment efficacy, it will not be discussed further.

Beyond the general lack of empirical support for these models, their usefulness is also ultimately limited by their reliance on correlational analyses. Model types 1 and 2 both depend on correlations between acoustic and physiological measures for their validity, but such correlations cannot demonstrate causation between a patient's physiological status and the acoustic variables used as indices of pathology. Thus, whatever relationship is observed between a measure and clinical status–a positive correlation, a negative correlation, no correlation, or a variable association– in the end tells us very little.

Finally, the stated or (more usually) assumed rationale behind measurements of jitter, shimmer, and noise is that irregular vibrations of the vocal folds, however caused, result in aperiodic acoustic signals, and that these measures will quantify such aperiodicities. This is reasonable enough on its face, but significant technical and theoretical issues emerge once measurement begins. A paradox underlies acoustic perturbation measurements: They are measures of signal aperiodicity, but implementation requires the assumption that a signal is periodic, because F0 must be very precisely tracked to accurately quantify such small cycle-to-cycle changes. Jitter, shimmer, and noise all cause changes in pulse shapes from cycle to cycle, making it difficult to identify a single landmark on a waveform with any confidence; and the more jitter and shimmer there are in a signal, the harder it is to measure them accurately. In fact, for voices that deviate from normal, measurement error may exceed the amount of jitter/shimmer present [36].[1] Further, listeners are not sensitive to changes in jitter and shimmer, which are not perceptually separable from other noise in the voice signal [38]. Finally, even if jitter and shimmer could be measured accurately, it is not possible to associate them with causes that are unambiguously attributable to disease processes. Perturbations in muscle innervation and/or in airflow, fluctuations in blood pressure across heartbeat cycles, mucous on the vocal folds, psychological stress [39], intentional use of creaky voice or breathiness to indicate group membership or intimacy (e.g., [40]), and/or phonemic uses of voice quality in many languages (e.g., [41]; see [42] for review) all add perturbation to voice signals, simultaneously with and indistinguishably from disease processes. Because jitter, shimmer, and noise all occur in normal speech —sometimes at high levels—it is arguable that such measures really tell us very little, if anything at all, about the presence or progression of Parkinson disease, or any other

---

[1] Attempts to circumvent such measurement problems by using spectral domain measures have generally been unsuccessful; see e.g. [37].

disease. These are bad properties for measurements to have, and jitter and shimmer have been largely abandoned in other studies of voice acoustics.

In summary, this review of the literature on acoustic measurement of voice in Parkinson disease leads to a singularly depressing conclusion. The choice of acoustic measures does not appear to be motivated by specific hypotheses or by any valid model of the disease, and measurement approaches have remained virtually unchanged for 60 years. Computational approaches have not improved this situation. Such studies may include thousands of measures in a "kitchen sink" approach, and make no claims, explicit or otherwise, about the relationship between the acoustic measures they use and what is being measured. Thus, although computational algorithms achieve good classification rates, they provide no insight into the physiological or perceptual basis of any observed differences between patients and control speakers, and thus no insight into the disease. Proposed solutions include seeking to standardize the methodological approach (e.g., [3]) or undertaking larger-scale studies (e.g., [43]), but not a shifting of focus to understand the cause/effect relationship between voice production (the cause), acoustics (the medium), and perception (the effect). In the end, research to date has provided no explanation for differences among speakers, over time, or across diagnostic groups. We are forced to conclude that whatever the goals of measurement, we know nothing at all about what acoustic variables to measure, or why.

3   Discussion

3.1   An Alternative Approach to Acoustic Assessment

All of the approaches to acoustic measurement of voice in Parkinson disease considered thus far have sought acoustic measures that are related to physiology, whether by examining differences between patients and control subjects or changes in voice as a result of treatment. However, because Parkinson disease is so variable both within and across patients, it remains unclear precisely what physiological details we are trying to capture with acoustic measures, so measures remain unmotivated and difficult to interpret. Clearly what is needed to resolve this situation is a model of the relationship between acoustics and physiology; but in the absence of theoretical or technical developments allowing more precise or better targeted measurement of a patient's physiological state (and without better acoustic measurements), how will such a model be developed?

One possibility is to use an alternative means of validating acoustic measures (other than by their association with voice physiology), and then seeking the physiological parameters associated with control of these validated measures. Acoustics stands between production and perception in the speech chain, so it is theoretically possible to motivate acoustic measures by beginning at either end of the chain: by demonstrating a causal association between an acoustic measure and some aspect of voice production, or by demonstrating a causal association between a measure or measures and voice quality and then examining the way in which speakers control perceptually-validated acoustic parameters. In the case of Parkinsonian dysphonia, we have argued above that this first approach is unlikely to bear fruit anytime soon; but what about an approach grounded in perception rather than production?

3.2   A Psychoacoustic Model of Voice Quality

Ideally, a psychoacoustic model of voice quality should include all the parameters needed to quantify the sound of a voice, and only those parameters. We have recently proposed such a model (Table 3; [44, 45]), which was developed by first identifying the acoustic attributes that vary the most from voice to voice [46] and then testing the perceptual significance of those parameters (e.g., [47, 48]). Finally, the model was validated by applying speech synthesis to evaluate the effectiveness of the set of parameters for modeling voice quality [49]. Over 200 voice samples (including more than 15 samples from individuals with Parkinson disease) have been evaluated by copy-synthesizing them using this psychoacoustic model, with the result that the synthetic voices were indistinguishable from the original target voice samples [50]. We therefore conclude that the model validly quantifies the voice disorders associated with Parkinson disease.

The features included in the psychoacoustic model are listed in Table 3. Following source-filter theory [51] they include formant frequencies and the associated bandwidths to model the vocal tract transfer function, and parameters to model the harmonic and inharmonic parts of the voice source (see e.g. [47] for derivation of these parameters). Additional parameters model F0, intensity, and their variability, consistent with classic psychoacoustic models of sound quality (e.g., [52]). Although this model was originally developed to model steady-state phonation, recent experiments suggest that it can be extended to continuous speech by the addition of measures of variability (e.g., coefficients of variation) for each parameter [45, 53].

Table 3. Parameters of the psychoacoustic model of voice quality. See [45] for details, including means and coefficients of variation for each parameter.

Parameters
Formant frequencies and bandwidths
F0 and intensity mean and contour
4 measures to parameterize the shape of the harmonic source spectrum
4 measures to parameterize the spectral shape of the inharmonic (noise) source

The final benefit of this approach to voice assessment is that it opens the way for physiopsychoacoustic modeling. Because we know these acoustic measures are perceptually important, they can serve as targets for studies of voice production, letting us ask questions about how speakers control perceptually-important acoustic parameters. This potentially resolves the issue of identifying which physical/physiological aspects of production are important, and can target treatment towards those aspects of voice production that have the most perceptual impact.

As a final note, recall that experimental approaches have not varied much in the past between studies examining treatment efficacy and those seeking to diagnose Parkinson disease or distinguish patients from control subjects. Both kinds of study use the same variables and similar analyses. The present reasoning suggests that these kinds of studies should differ. When the focus is on treatment efficacy, what really matters is the extent to which the treatment helps the patient communicate, project the correct self-image, and function socially. In contrast, the sound of the voice is of far less importance in studies seeking methods for early diagnosis of Parkinson disease, which are not critically dependent on the perceptibility of the variables used, or even on their particular motivation. In this case, accuracy is of more importance than theoretical motivation and parsimony, and the practical appeal of kitchen sink approaches may at present outweigh the concerns voiced above. With that said, accuracy can only improve when acoustic measures are well-matched to what they are intended to characterize, even in computational modeling, and better models of the relationships among voice perception, acoustics, and physiology can only benefit automatic detection systems.

4 Conclusions

Untangling the manner in which speakers control these acoustic parameters will not be an easy task, and an enormous amount of work will be required to uncover valid causal relationships between acoustic parameters and physiology. However, an enormous amount of effort has already been expended investigating acoustic measures of Parkinsonian dysphonia, with very little growth in understanding. In our belief, refocusing this effort by using perceptually validated acoustic measures as a basis for determining causal relations between acoustics and physiology offers hope for resolving the current impasse. At a minimum, we as a community must demand better motivation for measurement approaches, whether evaluating treatments or seeking to diagnose disease in its earliest stages.

Acknowledgements. This research was supported by NIH grant DC01797 and by NSF grant IIS-1704167.

Appendix

This appendix summarizes the acoustic measures used in the individual studies reviewed in this chapter.

Table 4. Acoustic measures included in individual studies reviewed in this paper. Numbers in the first column are those compiled in the last column of Table 2.

#	Ref.	Group	Acoustic measures	Why these variables?	Mechanism
1	Abeyesekera et al. 2019 [54]	2	F0 SD; intensity; jitter; shimmer; HNR	Not specified	Not specified
2	Alharbi et al. 2019 [34]	2	CPP, CPP SD; cepstral/spectral index of dysphonia; low/high spectral ratio	More robust than jitter	Increased glottal closure, subglottal pressure post-LSVT
3	Arora et al. 2019 [17]	1B	307 measures of F0, jitter, shimmer, HNR/NHR, GNE, vocal fold excitation ratio, glottis quotient, RPDE, DFA, PPE, EMD-ER, MFCCs, wavelet decomposition measures	Used in their previous studies	Not specified
4	Atkinson-Clement et al. 2015 [4]	3	F0; SPL	LSVT focus	Not specified
5	Azevedo et al. 2003 [55]	2	Many measures of F0; intensity mean/minimum/maximum; syllables/sec	Measures of prosody	Not specified
6	Bang et al. 2013 [8]	1A	Jitter %; shimmer dB; NHR; F1, F2	"The sensitive acoustic characteristics of vowel sounds" (p. 650)	Not specified
7	Bauer et al. 2011 [56]	1A	F0 minimum/maximum/range; jitter; shimmer; S/Z; MPT	Not specified	Respiratory mechanism deficiencies/glottal insufficiency
8	Bayestehtashk et al. 2015 [57]	1B	1582 features covering loudness, voicing, articulation	Not specified	Not specified
9	Benba et al. 2014 [58]	1B	20 PLP coefficients, 6 codebook sizes	Not specified	Not specified
10	Benba et al. 2016 [59]	1B	MFCCs; PLP coefficients; relative spectral PLP	Not specified	Not specified
11	Berus et al. 2018 [60]	1B	F0 mean/median/SD/minimum/maximum; 5 measures of jitter; 6 measures of shimmer; HNR, NHR; # unvoiced frames; # voice breaks; # pulses, # periods; autocorrelation	Not specified	Not specified
12	Canter 1963 [5]	1A	F0 median/range; SPL mean/range; rate, # pauses, mean pause length, mean phrase length, syllable duration	Description	Not specified
13	Canter 1965 [6]	1A	F0 range; SPL at 4 loudness levels; MPT	Relevant to physical support of phonation	Impaired control
14	Chenausky et al. 2011 [61]	1A	Syllable rate, syllable length variation, spirantization, VOT variation, vowel fraction	Not specified	Not specified
15	Cnockaert et al. 2008 [62]	1A	Modulation amplitude/frequency/energy ratio	Focus on tremor	Related to physiological tremor
16	Constantinescu et al. 2010 [63]	4	F0 range; SPL mean; MPT	LSVT focus	Not specified
17	Critchlely 1981 [64]	3	n/a	n/a	Impaired control of respiratory and laryngeal muscles
18	Cushnie-Sparrow et al. 2018 [10]	2	Jitter %; shimmer dB/%; HNR/CPP; spectral slope/trendline tilt; AVQI	Not specified	Not specified
19	D'Alatri et al. 2008 [65]	2	F0 mean/variability; amplitude variability; jitter %; shimmer %; NHR; tremor frequency/amplitude; DDK	Not specified	Not specified
20	Das 2010 [66]	1B	Not specified (compared 4 machine algorithms)	Not specified	Not specified
21	De Letter et al. 2010 [67]	2	F0 mean/CoV/variability in sentence; jitter; shimmer; HNR; F1, F2; DDK; syllable rate; tremor frequency/amplitude	Not specified	Might be due to respiratory muscle dysfunction
22	Dromey 2003 [68]	1A	F0 mean/SD, SPL, jitter, shimmer, HNR, LTAS	Not specified	Not specified

(*continued*)

Table 4. (*continued*)

#	Ref.	Group	Acoustic measures	Why these variables?	Mechanism
23	Dromey et al. 1995 [69]	4	F0 mean/SD/CoV; SPL/amplitude CoV; jitter; shimmer; HNR; harmonic spectral slope; friction duration, F2; MPT	LSVT focus	Not specified
24	Dromey et al. 2000 [70]	2	F0 mean/SD; SPL mean/SD; tremor index	Not specified	Not specified
25	Eskidere et al. 2012 [30]	1B	Jitter %/absolute/RAP/PPQ5/DDP; shimmer absolute/dB/APQ3/APQ5/APQ11/DDA; NHR/HNR; RPDE, DFA, PPE	Not specified	Not specified
26	Fabbri et al. 2017 [24]	2	F0 mean/SD; jitter mean/%; HNR; pitch break time, speech rate, vowel duration	Not specified	Not specified
27	Fenton 1982 [71]	4	Irregular waveforms (spectrographic analysis)	Not specified	Roughness caused by asymmetrical motion of vocal folds due to issues with muscle control
28	Flint et al. 1992 [72]	1A	F0 mean/SD/glide; F2 transitions, spirantization, VOT, voice intrusion errors; vowel duration, pause time mean/%	Not specified	Not specified
29	Forrest et al. 1989 [73]	1A	VOT	Focus on dysarthria/articulatory timing	Not specified
30	Fox et al. 2002 [32]	3	SPL	LSVT focus	(1) reduced neural drive to speech muscles; (2) a problem in perception of effort/inaccurate monitoring of vocal output, resulting in (3) difficulty using the right amount of effort to produce adequate loudness
31	Fox et al. 2006 [33]	3	SPL	LSVT focus	Poor kinesthetic feedback, leading to the wrong gain in motor control
32	Gamboa et al. 1997 [74]	1A	F0 mean/SD/range; intensity range/variability; jitter; shimmer; HNR; MPT, S/Z	Jitter and shimmer → stability of the phonatory system; SD of intensity and frequency → monopitch/monointensity	Not specified
				Not specified	
33	Gillivan-Murphy et al. 2019 [43]	1A	F0 CoV; amplitude CoV; periodicity; rate; tremor frequency/amplitude	Focus on tremor	Not specified
34	Goberman 2005 [75]	2	F0 mean/SD; intensity range; VSA; syll/sec; pause time	F0 mean → rigidity; F0 SD → VT stability	Different motor systems respond differently to DBS
35	Goberman and Coelho 2002 [20]	3	n/a	n/a	"Mechanisms incompletely understood" (p. 237)
36	Goberman and Coelho 2002 [76]	3	n/a	Shows variable effects of levodopa on voice	Not specified
37	Goberman et al. 2002 [77]	2	F0 mean/SD; intensity range	Not specified	Incr. in F0 → rigidity of laryngeal muscles; incr. F0 var → inability to maintain laryngeal muscles in fixed position
38	Goberman et al. 2005 [78]	2	F0 SD; pause time, speech rate, articulation rate	Not specified	Bradykinesia → reduced speech rates; levodopa → improved bradykinesia → increased speech rates
39	Goberman and Elmer 2005 [79]	1A	F0 mean/SD; F1, F2, VSA; articulation rate, % pause	Used in previous studies of clear speech	Not specified
40	Graças et al. 2012 [80]	1A	F0, jitter %/PPQ; shimmer %/APQ; HNR	Not specified	Not specified

(*continued*)

Table 4. (*continued*)

#	Ref.	Group	Acoustic measures	Why these variables?	Mechanism
41	Gustafsson et al. 2018 [81]	1A	F0; SPL; phonation time	LSVT focus	Standard LSVT model
42	Harel et al. 2004 [1]	4	F0 mean/variation	Related to stiffness due to dopamine depletion	Dopaminergic depletion causes muscle rigidity, increased laryngeal tension → decreased F0 range/variability.
43	Hariharan et al. 2014 [82]	1B	F0 mean/minimum/maximum; jitter %/absolute/RAP/PPQ/DDP; shimmer mean/dB/APQ/APQ3/APQ5/DDA; NHR, HNR; RPDE, D2, DFA, spread1 spread2, PPE	Used in previous studies	Not specified
44	Hertrich and Ackermann 1995 [26]	1A	F0; jitter; shimmer; HNR	Not specified	Not specified
45	Ho et al. 2008 [83]	2	Intensity mean/decay; duration	LSVT focus	Standard LSVT model
46	Hoffman-Ruddy et al. 2001 [84]	4	F0 mean/range; SPL; jitter %; shimmer %; HNR, VOT SD, MPT, syllables/sec, extended vowel durations	Not specified	Not specified
47	Holmes et al. 2000 [85]	1A	F0 mean/SD/range; intensity mean/SD; jitter; shimmer; NHR	Not specified	Not specified
48	Jiang et al. 1999 [86]	2	F0; SPL; jitter %; shimmer %; "peak performance ratio;" speed quotient	Measures of phonatory stability	Not specified
49	Jiménez-Jiménez 1997 [87]	1A	F0 mean/SD/range, intensity SD/range; jitter; shimmer; HNR; MPT, S/Z	"Stability of phonation system"	Not specified
50	Karlsson et al. 2013 [88]	2	F0 range/CoV	Interest in monopitch	Not specified
51	Kent et al. 2003 [39]	3	MDVP	Not specified	Not specified
52	Klostermann et al. 2008 [89]	2	F0; jitter; shimmer; NHR	Not specified	Not specified
53	Kompoliti et al. 2000 [28]	2	F0 mean/SD; jitter %; shimmer dB; HNR	Not specified	Rigidity
54	Lahmiri et al. 2018 [90]	1B	F0 mean/minimum/maximum; jitter %/absolute/RAP/PPQ/DDP; shimmer dB/%/APQ3/APQ5/MDVP APQ/DDA; NHR/HNR; RPDE, D2, PPE, DFA, nonlinear F0 measures	Used in previous studies	Not specified
55	Lazarus et al. 2012 [19]	1A	F0; SPL; MPT, S/Z, DDK	Not specified	Failure to control respiration → poor initiation of phonation/inability to raise loudness and vary pitch → monotonous, hoarse voice
56	Le Dorze et al. 1998 [91]	1A	F0 mean/SD/range; rate	Measures of prosody	Not specified
57	Lechien et al. 2018 [3]	3	n/a	n/a	n/a
58	Lee et al. 2008 [92]	2	F0 variability, amplitude variability, jitter %, shimmer %, HNR, D2	Not specified	Not specified
59	Little et al. 2009 [31]	1A	Jitter %/absolute/RAP/PPQ/DDP; shimmer absolute/dB/APQ/APQ3/APQ5/DDA; HNR/NHR; RPDE/DFA/D2/PPE	"Traditional" and "new"	Not specified
60	Majdinasab et al. 2016 [93]	1A	F0 mean/minimum/maximum/SD; jitter; shimmer; HNR	Not specified	Not specified
61	Majdinasab et al., 2017 [94]	2	F0 mean/SD; jitter; shimmer; HNR	Not specified	Not specified

(*continued*)

Table 4. *(continued)*

#	Ref.	Group	Acoustic measures	Why these variables?	Mechanism
62	Mate et al. 2012 [18]	2	F0 mean/SD, jitter; shimmer; HNR	Not specified	Not specified
63	Metter and Hanson 1986 [95]	1A	F0; relative intensity; rate, vowel phonation time	Not specified	Not specified
64	Midi et al. 2008 [23]	1A	F0 mean/variability; jitter %; shimmer %; NHR; DDK; MPT	Not specified	Dopaminergic depletion → rigidity of laryngeal muscles → increased laryngeal tension/decreased variability
65	Mourau 2005 [96]	2	F0; jitter/PPQ; shimmer/APQ; NHR	Not specified	Bradykinesia
66	Oguz et al. 2006 [97]	1A	F0; SPL; jitter; shimmer; HNR	Not specified	Not specified
67	Orozco-Arroyate et al. 2016 [98]	1B	4992 MFCC/GMM feature vectors; 256 prosodic features; 68 noise/F1/F2 features; 148 features related to unvoiced segments	Not specified	Not specified
68	Orozco-Arroyate et al. 2018 [99]	4	F0 mean/SD/maximum; energy mean/SD/maximum; jitter/PPQ; shimmer/APQ; degree unvoiced, VSA	Not specified	Not specified
69	Pinho et al. 2018 [25]	3	F0; intensity; jitter; shimmer; tremor	Not specified	Not specified
70	Rahn 2007 [100]	1A	Jitter %; shimmer %; D2	Not specified	Impaired function of the laryngeal, articulatory, and respiratory muscles
71	Ramig et al. 1988 [101]	1A	F0; jitter; shimmer; HNR	Sensitivity to instability	Not specified
72	Ramig et al. 2001 [102]	2	SPL	LSVT focus	Not specified
73	Ramig et al. 2001b [103]	2	F0 mean/SD; SPL	LSVT focus	"Mechanisms yet to be determined"; end up with standard LSVT rationale
74	Ramig et al. 2004 [104]	3	n/a	n/a	Deficits in internal cueing and sensory gating
75	Ramig 2018 [105]	2	SPL	LSVT focus	Standard LSVT model
76	Reyes et al. 2019 [106]	2	SPL; MPT	Related to respiration	Not specified
77	Romann et al. 2019 [107]	2	F0 mean/minimum/maximum/SD/CoV; jitter %/absolute/RAP/PPQ/smoothed PPQ; shimmer dB/%/CoV/amplitude/APQ/smoothed APQ; VTI, # subharmonic segs; #/degree voice breaks; #/degree unvoiced segments; F0 and amplitude tremor rates and extents	Not specified	Not specified
78	Rusz et al. 2011 [108]	1B	F0 SD; intensity SD, jitter local/RAP/PPQ5/DDP; shimmer local/APQ3/APQ5/APQ11/DDA; HNR/NHR; DDK rate/regularity, VOT, VSA, 4 other measures related to articulation; % pause time, articulatory rate, # pauses	"Traditional"	Not specified
79	Sakar et al. 2017 [16]	1B	Jitter %/absolute/RAP/PPQ5/DDP; shimmer absolute/dB/APQ3/APQ5/APQ11/DDA; NHR/HNR; RPDE; DFA; PPE	Not specified	Not specified
80	Sanabria et al. 2001 [109]	2	F0; jitter; shimmer; SPI, subharmonic segments; frequency tremor extent; voice breaks	Not specified	Not specified
81	Santos et al. 2010 [110]	1A	F0; jitter %; shimmer %; HNR, VTI	Not specified	Not specified

(continued)

Table 4. (*continued*)

#	Ref.	Group	Acoustic measures	Why these variables?	Mechanism
82	Sapir 2014 [35]	3	n/a	n/a	Standard LSVT framework
83	Schulz et al. 1999 [29]	2	F0, SPL; VOT; syllables/sec, syllable duration, MPT	Measures of pitch and loudness	Reduced rigidity, hypokinesia and tremor post-pallidotomy → changes in F0, SPL, etc.
84	Schulz et al. 2000 [111]	2	SPL	Not specified	Not specified
85	Searl et al. 2011 [112]	2	F0 mean/SD/range; intensity; MPT	Not specified	Not specified
86	Sewall et al. 2006 [113]	2	F0 range; SPL range; MPT	Not specified	Collagen reduces glottal gap
87	Sheibani et al. 2019 [114]	1B	F0 mean/minimum/maximum; jitter %/absolute/RAP/DDP, shimmer absolute/dB/APQ2/APQ5/APQ/DDA; HNR/NHR; RPDE, D2, DFA, spread1, spread2, PPE	Not specified	Not specified
88	Sidtis et al. 2010 [115]	2	HNR	"A measure of voice quality"	Not specified
89	Silbergleit et al. 2015 [116]	1A	F0 range; jitter; shimmer; HNR	Not specified	Not specified
90	Silva et al. 2012 [117]	1A	F0; jitter %; shimmer %; HNR	Not specified	Not specified
91	Skodda et al. 2010 [118]	2	F0 mean/SD; intensity; F1, F2; rate, pause ratio, pauses within words	Not specified	Not specified
92	Skodda et al. 2013 [119]	1A	F0 mean/SD; jitter; shimmer; NHR; F1, F2, VSA; speech rate, pause ratio, pauses within words	Not specified	Not specified
93	Stegemoller et al. 2017 [120]	2	F0 minimum/maximum; maximum intensity; duration	Not specified	Not specified
94	Tanaka et al. 2011 [121]	1A	F0 mean/CoV, jitter absolute/%/RAP, PPQ, SPPQ; shimmer dB/%/APQ/SAPQ/CoV; NHR, VTI, SPI, degree/number of subharmonics; degree/number voice breaks, rate/extent of frequency and amplitude tremor	Not specified	Not specified
95	Tanaka et al. 2015 [122]	2	F0; jitter %; shimmer %; NHR; degree of subharmonics; degree of voicelessness; amplitude and frequency tremor indices	Used before	Not specified
96	Tsanas et al. 2009 [123]	1A	Jitter %/absolute/RAP/PPQ/DDP; shimmer local/dB/APQ/APQ3/APQ5/DDA; HNR/NHR; RPDE, DFA, PPE	"Classic" measures; used before	Not specified
97	Tsanas, 2011 [124]	1A	Not precisely described (a 33-parameter model)	Kitchen sink	Not specified
98	Vaiciukynas et al. 2017 [9]	1B	18 sets of features; approximately 8700 in all	Kitchen sink	Not specified
99	Válalik et al. 2011 [125]	2	Jitter %; shimmer %; NHR; DFA; RPDE	Not specified	Not specified
100	Wight and Miller, 2015 [126]	2	Intensity	LSVT focus	Standard LSVT model
101	Wu et al. 2017 [127]	1B	F0 mean/minimum/maximum; jitter %/mean/RAP/PPQ/DDP; shimmer mean/dB/APQ3/APQ5/APQ11/DDA; HNR/NHR; RPDE, D2, DFA, 2 nonlinear measures of F0 variation, PPE	Not specified	Not specified

(*continued*)

Table 4. (*continued*)

#	Ref.	Group	Acoustic measures	Why these variables?	Mechanism
102	Xie et al. 2011 [128]	2	F0 mean/SD/CoV; amplitude variability; jitter %; shimmer %; NHR; F1, F2, F3; syllables/sec, DDK mean/CoV/jitter; frequency/amplitude tremor	Not specified	Not specified
103	Yücetürk et al. 2002 [129]	1A	F0 mean/minimum/maximum/range; intensity; HNR; MFT	Not specified	Not specified
104	Zhou et al. 2009 [130]	2	F0 variability; amplitude variability; jitter %; shimmer %; HNR, D2	Not specified	Not specified
105	Zwirner and Barnes 1992 [131]	1A	F0 SD; F1, F2	Phonatory/vocal tract stability	Not specified
106	Zwirner et al. 1991 [22]	1A	F0 mean/SD/range; jitter; shimmer %; HNR	Not specified	Not specified

References

1. Harel, B., Cannizzaro, M., Snyder, P.J.: Variability in fundamental frequency during speech in prodromal and incipient Parkinson's disease: a longitudinal case study. Brain Cogn. **56**, 24–29 (2004)

2. Catford, J.C.: Fundamental Problems in Phonetics. Edinburgh University Press, Edinburgh (1977)

3. Lechien, J.R., et al.: Voice quality outcomes of idiopathic Parkinson's disease medical treatment: a systematic review. Clin. Otolaryngol. **43**, 882–903 (2018)

4. Atkinson-Clement, C., Sadat, J., Pinto, S.: Behavioral treatments for speech in Parkinson's disease: meta-analyses and review of the literature. Neurodegener. Dis. Manag. **5**, 233–248 (2015)

5. Canter, G.J.: Speech characteristics of patients with Parkinson's disease. I. Intensity, pitch, and duration. J. Speech Hear. Disord. **28**, 221–229 (1963)

6. Canter, G.J.: Speech characteristics of patients with Parkinson's disease: II. Physiological support for speech. J. Speech Hear. Disord. **30**, 44–49 (1965)

7. Milenkovic, P., Read, C.: CSpeech Supplement User's Manual, CSpeech Version 3.1. Author, Madison, WI (1990)

8. Bang, Y., Minc, K., Sohnd, Y.H., Cho, S.: Acoustic characteristics of vowel sounds in patients with Parkinson disease. NeuroRehabilitation **32**, 649–654 (2013)

9. Vaiciukynas, E., Verikas, A., Gelzinis, A., Bacauskiene, M.: Detecting Parkinson's disease from sustained phonation and speech signals. PLoS ONE **12**, e0185613 (2017)

10. Cushnie-Sparrow, D., Adams, S., Abeyesekera, A., Pieterman, M., Gilmore, G., Jog, M.: Voice quality severity and responsiveness to levodopa in Parkinson's disease. J. Commun. Disord. **76**, 1–10 (2018)

11. Ramig, L., Fox, C., Sapir, S.: Speech treatment for Parkinson's disease. Expert Rev. Neurother. **8**, 297–309 (2008)

12. Buder, E.: Acoustic analysis of voice quality: a tabulation of algorithms 1902-1990. In: Kent, R.D., Ball, M.J. (eds.) Voice Quality Measurement, pp. 119–244. Singular, San Diego (2000)

13. Hillenbrand, J., Houde, R.A.: Acoustic correlates of breathy vocal quality: dysphonic voices and continuous speech. J. Speech Hear. Res. **39**, 311–321 (1996)

14. Herzel, H., Berry, D., Titze, I., Saleh, M.: Analysis of vocal disorders with methods from nonlinear dynamics. J. Speech Hear. Res. **37**, 1008–1119 (1994)

15. Baken, R.J., Orlikoff, R.: Clinical Measurement of Voice and Speech. Singular, San Diego, CA (2000)
16. Sakar, B.E., Serbes, G., Sakar, C.O.: Analyzing the effectiveness of vocal features in early telediagnosis of Parkinson's disease. PLoS ONE **12**, e0182428 (2017)
17. Arora, S., Baghai-Ravary, L., Tsanas, A.: Developing a large scale population screening tool for the assessment of Parkinson's disease using telephone-quality voice. J. Acoust. Soc. Am. **145**, 2871–2884 (2019)
18. Mate, M.A., Cobeta, I., Jiménez-Jiménez, F.J., Figueiras, R.: Digital voice analysis in patients with advanced Parkinson's disease undergoing deep brain stimulation therapy. J. Voice **26**, 496–501 (2012)
19. Lazarus, J.P., et al.: A study of voice profiles and acoustic signs in patients with Parkinson's disease in North India. J. Clin. Neurosci. **19**, 1125–1129 (2012)
20. Goberman, A., Coelho, C.: Acoustic analysis of Parkinsonian speech I: speech characteristics and L-dopa therapy. NeuroRehabilitation **17**, 237–246 (2002)
21. Zhang, Y., Jiang, J., Rahn, D.A.: Studying vocal fold vibrations in Parkinson's disease with a nonlinear model. Chaos **15**, 033903 (2005)
22. Zwirner, P., Murry, T., Woodson, G.: Phonatory function of neurologically impaired patients. J. Commun. Disord. **24**, 287–300 (1991)
23. Midi, I., Dogan, M., Koseoglu, M., Can, G., Sehitoglu, M.A., Gunal, D.I.: Voice abnormalities and their relation with motor dysfunction in Parkinson's disease. Acta Neurol. Scand. **117**, 26–34 (2008)
24. Fabbri, M., et al.: Speech and voice response to a levodopa challenge in late-stage Parkinson's disease. Front. Neurol. **8**, 432 (2017)
25. Pinho, P., Monteiro, L., Soares, M., Tourinho, L., Melo, A., Nobrega, A.C.: Impact of levodopa treatment in the voice pattern of Parkinson's disease patients: a systematic review and meta-analysis. CoDAS **30**, e20170200 (2018)
26. Hertrich, I., Ackermann, H.: Gender-specific vocal dysfunctions in Parkinson's disease: electroglottographic and acoustic analyses. Ann. Otol. Rhinol. Laryngol. **104**, 197–202 (1995)
27. Baumgartner, C.A., Sapir, S., Ramig, L.: Voice quality changes following phonatory-respiratory effort treatment (LSVT) versus respiratory effort treatment for individuals with Parkinson disease. J. Voice **15**, 105–114 (2001)
28. Kompoliti, K., Wang, Q.E., Goetz, C.G., Leurgans, S., Raman, R.: Effects of central dopaminergic stimulation by apomorphine on speech in Parkinson's disease. Neurology **54**, 458–462 (2000)
29. Schulz, G.M., Peterson, T., Sapienza, C.M., Greer, M., Friedman, W.: Voice and speech characteristics of persons with Parkinon's disease pre- and post-pallidotomy surgery: preliminary findings. J. Speech Lang. Hear. Res. **42**, 1176–1194 (1999)
30. Eskidere, Ö., Ertaş, F., Hanilçi, C.: A comparison of regression methods for remote tracking of Parkinson's disease progression. Expert Syst. Appl. **39**, 5523–5528 (2012)
31. Little, M.A., McSharry, P.E., Roberts, S.J., Costello, D.A.E., Moroz, I.M.: Exploiting nonlinear recurrence and fractal scaling properties for voice disorder detection. Biomed. Eng. Online **6**, 23 (2009)
32. Fox, C.M., Morrison, C.E., Ramig, L., Sapir, S.: Current perspectives on the Lee Silverman voice treatment (LSVT) for individuals with idiopathic Parkinson disease. Am. J. Speech-Lang. Pathol **11**, 111–123 (2002)
33. Fox, C.M., Ramig, L., Ciucci, M.R., Sapir, S., McFarland, D.H., Farley, B.G.: The science and practice of LSVT/LOUD: neural plasticity–principled approach to treating individuals with Parkinson disease and other neurological disorders. Semin. Speech Lang. **27**, 283–299 (2006)

34. Alharbi, G.G., Cannito, M.P., Buder, E.H., Awan, S.N.: Spectral/cepstral analyses of phonation in Parkinson's disease before and after voice treatment: a preliminary study. Folia Phoniatr. Logop. **71**, 275–285 (2019)

35. Sapir, S.: Multiple factors are involved in the dysarthria associated with Parkinson's disease: a review with implications for clinical practice and research. J. Speech Lang. Hear. Res. **57**, 1330–1343 (2014)

36. Gerratt, B.R., Kreiman, J.: Utility of acoustic measures of voice. In: Proceedings of the Workshop on Standardization in Acoustic Voice Analysis, pp. GER1 - GER7. National Center for Voice and Speech, Denver (1995)

37. Murphy, P.J.: Spectral noise estimation in the evaluation of pathological voice. Logop. Phoniatr. Vocol. **31**, 182–189 (2006)

38. Kreiman, J., Gerratt, B.R.: Perception of aperiodicity in pathological voice. J. Acoust. Soc. Am. **117**, 2201–2211 (2005)

39. Kent, R.D., Vorperian, H.K., Kent, J.F., Duffy, J.R.: Voice dysfunction in dysarthria: application of the multi-dimensional voice program. J. Commun. Disord. **36**, 281–306 (2003)

40. Yuasa, I.P.: Creaky voice: a new feminine voice quality for young urban-oriented upwardly mobile American women? Am. Speech **85**, 315–337 (2010)

41. Garellek M.: Acoustic discriminability of the complex phonation system in !Xóõ. Phonetica **77**, 131–160 (2020)

42. Kreiman, J., Sidtis, D.: Foundations of Voice Studies. Wiley-Blackwell, Malden, MA (2011)

43. Gillivan-Murphy, P., Miller, N., Carding, P.: Voice tremor in Parkinson's disease: an acoustic study. J. Voice **33**, 526–535 (2019)

44. Kreiman, J., Gerratt, B.R., Garellek, M., Samlan, R., Zhang, Z.: Toward a unified theory of voice production and perception. Loquens **1**, e009 (2014)

45. Lee, C.Y., Keating, P., Kreiman, J.: Acoustic voice variation within and between speakers. J. Acoust. Soc. Am. **146**, 1568–1579 (2019)

46. Kreiman, J., Gerratt, B.R., Antoñanzas-Barroso, N.: Measures of the glottal source spectrum. J. Speech Lang. Hear. Res. **50**, 595–610 (2007)

47. Kreiman, J., Gerratt, B.R.: Perceptual interactions of the harmonic source and noise in voice. J. Acoust. Soc. Am. **131**, 492–500 (2012)

48. Garellek, M., Samlan, R., Gerratt, B.R., Kreiman, J.: Modeling the voice source in terms of spectral slopes. J. Acoust. Soc. Am. **139**, 1404–1410 (2016)

49. Kreiman, J., Gerratt, B.R., Signorello, R., Rastifar, S.: Sufficiency of a four-parameter spectral model of the voice source. J. Acoust. Soc. Am. **137**, 2266 (2015)

50. Kreiman, J., Lee, C.Y., Garellek, M., Samlan, R., Gerratt, B.R.: Validating a psychoacoustic model of voice quality. J. Acoust. Soc. Am. (2021, to appear)

51. Fant, G.: Acoustic Theory of Speech Production. Mouton, The Hague (1960)

52. Fastl, H.: The psychoacoustics of sound-quality evaluation. Acta Acustica United Acustica **83**, 754–764 (1997)

53. Gerratt, B.R., Kreiman, J., Garellek, M.: Comparing measures of voice quality from sustained phonation and continuous speech. J. Speech Lang. Hear. Res. **59**, 994–1001 (2016)

54. Abeyesekera, A., et al.: Effects of deep brain stimulation of the subthalamic nucleus settings on voice quality, intensity, and prosody in Parkinson's disease: preliminary evidence for speech optimization. Can. J. Neurol. Sci. **46**, 287–294 (2019)

55. Azevedo, L.L., Cardoso, F., Reis, C.: Acoustic analysis of prosody in females with Parkinson's disease: comparison with normal controls. Arq. Neuropsiquiatr. **61**, 999–1003 (2003)

56. Bauer, V., Alerić, Z., Jančić, E., Miholović, V.: Voice quality in Parkinson's disease in the Croatian language speakers. Collegium Antropologicum **35**(Suppl. 2), 209–212 (2011)

57. Bayestehtashka, A., Asgaria, M., Shafrana, I., McNames, J.: Fully automated assessment of the severity of Parkinson's disease from speech. Comput. Speech Lang. **29**, 172–185 (2015)

58. Benba, A., Jilbab, A., Hammouch, A.: Voice analysis for detecting persons with Parkinson's disease using PLP and VQ. J. Theor. Appl. Inf. Technol. **70**, 443–450 (2014)

59. Benba, A., Jilbab, A., Hammouch, A.: Discriminating between patients with Parkinson's and neurological diseases using cepstral analysis. IEEE Trans. Neural Syst. Rehabil. Eng. **24**, 1100–1108 (2016)

60. Berus, L., Klancnik, S., Brezocnik, M., Ficko, M.: Classifying Parkinson's disease based on acoustic measures using artificial neural networks. Sensors (Basel) **19**(1), 16 (2018)

61. Chenausky, K., MacAuslan, J., Goldhor, R.: Acoustic analysis of PD speech. Parkinsons Dis. 2011, Article ID 435232 (2011)

62. Cnockaert, L., Schoentgen, J., Auzou, P., Ozsancak, C., Defebvre, L., Grenez, F.: Low-frequency vocal modulations in vowels produced by Parkinsonian subjects. Speech Commun. **50**, 288–300 (2008)

63. Constantinescu, G.A., Theodoros, D.G., Russel, T.G., Ward, E.C., Wilson, S.J., Wootton, R.: Homebased speech treatment for Parkinson's disease delivered remotely: a case report. J. Telemed. Telecare **16**, 100–104 (2010)

64. Critchlely, E.M.R.: Speech disorders of Parkinsonism: a review. J. Neurol. Neurosurg. Psychiat. **44**, 751–758 (1981)

65. D'Alatri, L., Paludetti, G., Contarino, M.F., Galla, S., Marchese, M.R., Bentivoglio, A.R.: Effects of bilateral subthalamic nucleus stimulation and medication on Parkinsonian speech impairment. J. Voice **22**, 365–372 (2008)

66. Das, R.: A comparison of multiple classification methods for diagnosis of Parkinson disease. Expert Syst. Appl. **37**, 1568–1572 (2010)

67. De Letter, M., Van Borsel, J., Boon, P., De Bodt, M., Dhooge, I., Santens, P.: Sequential changes in motor speech across a levodopa cycle in advanced Parkinson's disease. Int. J. Speech-Lang. Pathol. **12**, 405–413 (2010)

68. Dromey, C.: Spectral measures and perceptual ratings of hypokinetic dysarthria. J. Med. Speech Lang. Pathol. **11**, 85–94 (2003)

69. Dromey, C., Ramig, L., Johnson, A.B.: Phonatory and articulatory changes associated with increased vocal intensity in Parkinson disease: a case study. J. Speech Hear. Res. **38**, 751–764 (1995)

70. Dromey, C., Kumar, R., Lang, A.E., Lozano, A.M.: An investigation of the effects of subthalamic nucleus stimulation on acoustic measures of voice. Mov. Disord. **15**, 1132–1138 (2000)

71. Fenton, E., Schley, W.S., Niimi, S.: Vocal symptoms in Parkinson disease treated with levodopa: a case report. Ann. Otol. **91**, 119–121 (1982)

72. Flint, A.J., Black, S.E., Campbell-Taylor, I., Gailey, G.F., Levinton, C.: Acoustic analysis in the differentiation of Parkinson's disease and major depression. J. Psycholinguist. Res. **21**, 383–399 (1992)

73. Forrest, K., Weismer, G., Turner, G.S.: Kinematic, acoustic, and perceptual analyses of connected speech produced by Parkinsonian and normal geriatric adults. J. Acoust. Soc. Am. **85**, 2608–2622 (1989)

74. Gamboa, J., et al.: Acoustic voice analysis in patients with Parkinsons disease treated with dopaminergic drugs. J. Voice **11**, 314–320 (1997)

75. Goberman, A.: Correlation between acoustic speech characteristics and non-speech motor performance in Parkinson disease. Med. Sci. Monit. **11**, 109–116 (2005)

76. Goberman, A., Coelho, C.: Acoustic analysis of Parkinsonian speech II: L-dopa related fluctuations and methodological issues. NeuroRehabilitation **17**, 247–254 (2002)

77. Goberman, A., Coelho, C., Robb, M.: Phonatory characteristics of Parkinsonian speech before and after morning medication: the ON and OFF states. J. Commun. Disord. **35**, 217–239 (2002)

78. Goberman, A., Coelho, C., Robb, M.: Prosodic characteristics of Parkinsonian speech: the effect of levodopa-based medication. J. Med. Speech-Lang. Pathol. **13**, 51–68 (2005)

79. Goberman, A., Elmer, L.W.: Acoustic analysis of clear versus conversational speech in individuals with Parkinson disease. J. Commun. Disord. **38**, 215–230 (2005)

80. Graças, R., Gama, A., Cardoso, F., Lopes, B., Bassi, I.: Objective and subjective analysis of women's voice with idiopathic Parkinson's disease. Arq. Neuropsiquiatr. **70**, 492–496 (2012)

81. Gustafsson, J.K., Södersten, M., Ternström, S., Schalling, E.: Long-term effects of Lee Silverman voice treatment on daily voice use in Parkinson's disease as measured with a portable voice accumulator. Logop. Phoniatr. Vocol. **44**, 124–133 (2018)

82. Hariharan, M., Polat, K., Sindhu, R.: A new hybrid intelligent system for accurate detection of Parkinson's disease. Comput. Meth. Programs Biomed. **113**, 904–913 (2014)

83. Ho, A.K., Bradshaw, J.L., Iansek, R.: For better or worse: the effect of levodopa on speech in Parkinson's disease. Mov. Disord. **23**, 574–580 (2008)

84. Hoffman-Ruddy, B., Schulz, G., Vitek, J., Evatt, M.: A preliminary study of the effects of subthalamic nucleus (STN) deep brain stimulation (DBS) on voice and speech characteristics in Parkinson's disease (PD). Clin. Linguist. Phon. **15**, 97–101 (2008)

85. Holmes, R.J., Oates, J.M., Phyland, D.J., Hughes, A.J.: Voice characteristics in the progression of Parkinson's disease. Int. J. Lang. Commun. Disord. **35**, 407–418 (2000)

86. Jiang, J., Lin, E., Wang, J., Hanson, D.G.: Glottographic measures before and after levodopa treatment in Parkinson's disease. Laryngoscope **109**, 1287–1294 (1999)

87. Jiménez-Jiménez, F.J., et al.: Acoustic voice analysis in untreated patients with Parkinson's disease. Parkinsonism Relat. Disord. **3**, 111–116 (1997)

88. Karlsson, F., Olofsson, K., Blomstedt, P., Linder, J., van Doorn, J.: Pitch variability in patients with Parkinson's disease: effects of deep brain stimulation of caudal zona incerta and subthalamic nucleus. J. Speech Lang. Hear. Res. **56**, 1–9 (2013)

89. Klostermann, F., et al.: Effects of subthalamic deep brain stimulation on dysarthrophonia in Parkinson's disease. J. Neurol. Neurosurg. Psychiatry **79**, 522–529 (2008)

90. Lahmiri, S., Dawson, D.A., Shmuel, A.: Performance of machine learning methods in diagnosing Parkinson's disease based on dysphonia measures. Biomed. Eng. Lett. **8**(1), 29–39 (2017). https://doi.org/10.1007/s13534-017-0051-2

91. Le Dorze, G., Ryall, J., Brassard, C., Boulanger, N., Ratté, D.: A comparison of the prosodic characteristics of the speech of people with Parkinson's disease and Friedreich's ataxia with neurologically normal speakers. Folia Phoniatr. Logop. **50**, 1–9 (1998)

92. Lee, V.S., Zhou, X.P., Rahn, D., Wang, E.Q., Jiang, J.: Perturbation and nonlinear dynamic analysis of acoustic phonatory signal in Parkinsonian patients receiving deep brain stimulation. J. Commun. Disord. **41**, 485–500 (2008)

93. Majdinasab, F., Karkheiran, S., Soltani, M., Moradi, N., Shahidi, G.: Relationship between voice and motor disabilities of Parkinson's disease. J. Voice **30**(768), e17–768.e22 (2016)

94. Majdinasab, F., Khatoonabadi, A., Khoddami, S.M., Habibi, A.: The effect of bilateral subthalamic nucleus deep brain stimulation (STN-DBS) on the acoustic and prosodic features in patients with Parkinson's disease: a study protocol for the first trial on Iranian patients. Med. J. Islam. Repub. Iran **31**, 118 (2017)

95. Metter, E.J., Hanson, W.R.: Clinical and acoustical variability in hypokinetic dysarthria. J. Commun. Disord. **19**, 347–366 (1986)

96. Mourau, L., Aguiar, P., Ferraz, F., Behlau, M., Ferraz, H.: Acoustic voice assessment in Parkinson's disease patients submitted to posteroventral pallidotomy. Arq. Neuropsiquiatr. **63**, 20–25 (2005)

97. Oguz, H., Tunc, T., Safak, M.A., Inan, L., Kargin, S., Demirci, M.: Objective voice changes in nondysphonic Parkinson's disease patients. J. Otolaryngol. **35**, 349–354 (2006)

98. Orozco-Arroyave, J.R., et al.: Automatic detection of Parkinson's disease in running speech spoken in three different languages. J. Acoust. Soc. Am. **139**, 481–500 (2016)

99. Orozco-Arroyave, J.R., et al.: NeuroSpeech: an open-source software for Parkinson's speech analysis. Digit. Signal Process. **77**, 207–221 (2018)

100. Rahn, D.A., Chou, M., Jiang, J.J., Zhang, Y.: Phonatory impairment in Parkinson's disease: evidence from nonlinear dynamics analysis and perturbation analysis. J. Voice **21**, 64–71 (2007)

101. Ramig, L., Scherer, R., Titze, I., Ringel, S.: Acoustic analysis of voices of patients with neurologic disease: rationale and preliminary data. Ann. Otol. Rhinol. Laryngol. **97**, 164–172 (1988)

102. Ramig, L., Sapir, S., Fox, C., Countryman, S.: Changes in vocal loudness following intensive voice treatment (LSVT) in individuals with Parkinson's disease: a comparison with untreated patients and normal age-matched controls. Mov. Disord. **16**, 79–83 (2001)

103. Ramig, L., et al.: Intensive voice treatment (LSVT) for patients with Parkinson's disease: a 2 year follow up. J. Neurol. Neurosurg. Psychiatry **71**, 493–498 (2001)

104. Ramig, L., Fox, C., Sapir, S.: Parkinson's disease: speech and voice disorders and their treatment with the Lee Silverman voice treatment. Semin. Speech Lang. **25**, 169–180 (2004)

105. Ramig, L., Halpern, A., Spielman, J., Fox, C., Freeman, K.: Speech treatment in Parkinson's disease: randomized controlled trial (RCT). Mov. Disord. **33**, 1777–1791 (2018)

106. Reyes, A., Castillo, A., Castillo, J., Cornejo, I., Cruickshank, T.: The effects of respiratory muscle training on phonatory measures in individuals with Parkinson's disease. J. Voice **34**, 894–902 (2020)

107. Romann, A.J., Beber, B.C., Cielo, C.A., Rieder, C.: Acoustic voice modifications in individuals with Parkinson disease submitted to deep brain stimulation. Int. Arch. Otorhinolaryngol. **23**, 203–208 (2019)

108. Rusz, J., Cmejla, R., Ruzickova, H., Ruzicka, E.: Quantitative acoustic measurements for characterization of speech and voice disorders in early untreated Parkinson's disease. J. Acoust. Soc. Am. **129**, 350–367 (2011)

109. Sanabria, J., et al.: The effect of levodopa on vocal function in Parkinson's disease. Clin. Neuropharmacol. **24**, 99–102 (2001)

110. Santos, L., et al.: Acoustic and hearing-perceptual voice analysis in individuals with idiopathic Parkinson's disease in "on" and "off" stages. Arq. Neuropsiquiatr. **68**, 706–711 (2010)

111. Schulz, G.M., Greer, M., Friedman, W.: Changes in vocal intensity in Parkinson's disease following pallidotomy surgery. J. Voice **14**, 589–606 (2000)

112. Searl, J., Wilson, K., Haring, K.: Feasibility of group voice therapy for individuals with Parkinson's disease. J. Commun. Disord. **44**, 719–732 (2011)

113. Sewall, G.K., Jiang, J.J., Ford, C.N.: Clinical evaluation of Parkinson's-related dysphonia. Laryngoscope **116**, 1740–1744 (2006)

114. Sheibani, R., Mkookar, E., Alavi, S.E.: An ensemble method for diagnosis of Parkinson's disease based on voice measurements. J. Med. Signals Sens. **9**, 221–226 (2019)

115. Sidtis, D., Rogers, T., Godier, V., Tagliati, M., Sidtis, J.J.: Voice and fluency changes as a function of speech task and deep brain stimulation. J. Speech Lang. Hear. Res. **53**, 1167–1177 (2010)
116. Silbergleit, A.K., LeWitt, P.A., Peterson, E.L., Gardner, G.M.: Quantitative analysis of voice in Parkinson disease compared to motor performance: a pilot study. J. Parkinson's Dis. **5**, 517–524 (2015)
117. Silva, L., Gama, A.C., Cardoso, F., Reis, C., Bassi, I.: Idiopathic Parkinson's disease: vocal and quality of life analysis. Arq. Neuropsiquiatr. **70**, 674–679 (2012)
118. Skodda, S., Visser, W., Schlegel, U.: Short- and long-term dopaminergic effects on dysarthria in early Parkinson's disease. J. Neural Transm. **117**, 197–205 (2010)
119. Skodda, S., Grönheit, W., Mancinelli, N., Schlegel, U.: Progression of voice and speech impairment in the course of Parkinson's disease: a longitudinal study. Parkinson's Dis. 2013, Article ID 389195 (2013)
120. Stegemöller, E.L., Radig, H., Hibbing, P., Wingate, J., Sapienza, C.: Effects of singing on voice, respiratory control and quality of life in persons with Parkinson's disease. Disabil. Rehabil. **39**, 594–600 (2017)
121. Tanaka, Y., Nishio, M., Niimi, S.: Vocal acoustic characteristics of patients with Parkinson's disease. Folia Phoniatr. Logop. **63**, 223–230 (2011)
122. Tanaka, Y., et al.: Voice features of Parkinson's disease patients with subthalamic nucleus deep brain stimulation. J. Neurol. **262**(5), 1173–1181 (2015). https://doi.org/10.1007/s00415-015-7681-z
123. Tsanas, A., Little, M.A., McSharry, P.E., Ramig, L.: Accurate telemonitoring of Parkinson's disease progression by non-invasive speech tests. IEEE Trans. Biomed. Eng. **57**, 884–893 (2009)
124. Tsanas, A., Little, M.A., McSharry, P.E., Ramig, L.: Nonlinear speech analysis algorithms mapped to a standard metric achieve clinically useful quantification of average Parkinson's disease symptom severity. J. Roy. Soc. Interface **8**, 842–855 (2011)
125. Valálik, I., Smehák, G., Bognár, L., Csókay, A.: Voice acoustic changes during bilateral subthalamic stimulation in patients with Parkinson's disease. Clin. Neurol. Neurosurg. **113**, 188–195 (2011)
126. Wight, S., Miller, N.: Lee Silverman voice treatment for people with Parkinson's: audit of outcomes in a routine clinic. Int. J. Lang. Commun. Disord. **50**, 215–225 (2015)
127. Wu, Y., et al.: Dysphonic voice pattern analysis of patients in Parkinson's disease using minimum interclass probability risk feature selection and bagging ensemble learning methods. Comput. Math. Meth. Med. 2017, Article ID 4201984 (2017)
128. Xie, Y., Zhang, Y., Zheng, Z., et al.: Changes in speech characters of patients with Parkinson's disease after bilateral subthalamic nucleus stimulation. J. Voice **25**, 751–758 (2011)
129. Yücetürk, A.V., Yilmaz, H., Eğrilmez, M., Karaca, S.: Voice analysis and videolaryngostroboscopy in patients with Parkinson's disease. Eur. Arch. Otorhinolaryngol. **259**, 290–293 (2002)
130. Zhou, X.P., Lee, V.S., Wang, E.Q., Jiang, J.J.: Evaluation of the effects of deep brain stimulation of the subthalamic nucleus and levodopa treatment on Parkinsonian voice using perturbation, nonlinear dynamic, and perceptual analysis. Folia Phoniatr. Logop. **61**, 189–199 (2009)
131. Zwirner, P., Barnes, G.J.: Vocal tract steadiness: a measure of phonatory and upper airway motor control during phonation in dysarthria. J. Speech Hear. Res. **35**, 761–768 (1992)
132. Ma, A., Lau, K., Thyagarajan, D.: Voice changes in Parkinson's disease: what are they telling us? J. Clin. Neurosci. preprint ahead of publication (2020)

Sources of Intraspeaker Variation in Parkinsonian Speech Related to Speaking Style

Jason A. Whitfield$^{(\boxtimes)}$ ⓘ

Bowling Green State University, Bowling Green, OH 43402, USA
jawhitf@bgsu.edu

Abstract. Data from several studies suggest that individuals with PD exhibit improvements in motor control when cued to increase attention and effort when performing several activities of daily living. The variability in speech motor impairment reported across studies and patients may be influenced by the extent to which a speaker relies more heavily on either goal-directed or habitual control in a given speaking environment. The current paper will briefly review changes in acoustic features of articulation associated with adopting more goal-directed speaking styles such a clear or loud speech and discuss related implications for the automatic assessment of parkinsonian speech.

Keywords: Parkinsonian speech · Speech acoustics · Speech articulation

1 Introduction

Parkinson disease (PD) is the second most prevalent progressive neurological disease, affecting approximately 1% of the population over the age of 60 (Hirtz et al. 2007; de Lau and Breteler 2006; Wirdefeldt, Adami, Cole, Trichopoulos, and Mandel 2011). The classic motor deficits, including bradykinesia (slowness), rigidity (increased resistance to passive stretch), akinesia (difficulty initiating movement), and hypokinesia (reduced range of movement), along with tremor and postural instability, are largely thought to arise from basal ganglia dysfunction associated with the loss of dopaminergic input from the substantia nigra pars compacta. For most patients, between 70–90% of the dopaminergic neurons in this midbrain region have degenerated by the onset of motor symptoms and diagnosis (e.g., Dickson et al. 2008; Fearnley and Lees 1991; Lang and Lozano 1998; Rabey and Burns 2008; Rodriguez-Oroz et al. 2009). Selective degeneration of these cells leads to dysfunction of the dorsolateral striatum, which is largely involved with the implementation of habitual action and overlearned responses (e.g., Damier, Hirsch, Agid, and Graybiel 1999; Kish, Shannak, and Hornykiewicz 1998; Redgrave et al. 2010; Wu et al. 2012). Neuroanatomical studies suggest PD is associated with a more systemic pathology that eventually progresses to affect these dopamine-producing cells, indicating that there is likely a prodromal phase of the disease that precedes the onset of the classic motor deficits (e.g., Braak Ghebremedhin, Rüb, Bratzke, and del Tredici 2004).

J. I. Godino-Llorente (Ed.): AAPS 2019, CCIS 1295, pp. 24–41, 2020.
https://doi.org/10.1007/978-3-030-65654-6_2

The classic motor deficits associated with PD extend to the speech motor system, leading to a cluster of symptoms consistent with hypokinetic dysarthria (e.g., Darley, Aronson, and Brown 1969a, 1969b). It is estimated that 70 to 90 percent of individuals with PD exhibit some degree of speech motor impairment, with nearly 100% of patients experiencing changes in speech and voice throughout the course of the disease (e.g., Ho, Iansek, Marigliani, Bradshaw, and Gates 1999; Logemann, Fisher, Boshes, and Blonsky 1978). The most common perceptual deficits associated with dysarthria in PD include phonatory, articulatory, and prosodic insufficiencies (e.g., Darley et al. 1969b; Logemann et al. 1978). Phonatory impairment is most often characterized by reduced vocal loudness accompanied by a rough and/or breathy voice quality. Articulatory impairment is typically characterized by consonant imprecision, short rushes of speech, and speech disfluency. Prosodic impairment is characterized by reduced syllabic stress, monopitch, monoloudness, and pause abnormalities (e.g., Darley et al. 1969b; Logemann et al. 1978; Sapir 2014). Recent advances in digital signal processing and machine learning have opened up a wide range of possibilities for detecting changes in voice and speech associated with PD, to enhance diagnostic and prognostic indicators of disease onset and progression (e.g., Galaz et al. 2016; Orozco-Arroyave et al. 2016; Tsanas, A., Little, M. A., McSharry, P. E., Spielman, J., and Ramig 2012; Vásquez-Correa et al. 2019).

While it is well known that PD affects several aspects of speech production, recent work in the fields of basic neuroscience and speech motor control suggest that the nature of dysarthria in PD is multifactorial (see Sapir 2014). Therefore, the nature of basal ganglia dysfunction in PD holds important implications for augmenting our understanding of speech motor impairment in parkinsonian speech. The basal ganglia is a series of interconnected subcortical nuclei that make a series of re-entrant loops with the cortex (e.g., Alexander, DeLong, and Strick 1986; Redgrave et al. 2010). The primary input to the basal ganglia is the corpus striatum, which is comprised of the putamen, caudate nucleus, and nucleus accumbens. Across its body, the striatum receives synaptic input from nearly all regions of the cortex and several subcortical regions. The sensitivity of these inputs are modulated by several interneuron connections within the striatum and by dopaminergic input from the substantia nigra pars compacta and the ventral tegmental area in the midbrain. The basal ganglia include several inhibitory connections between the striatum, the internal and external segments of the globus pallidus, subthalamic nuclei, substantia nigra pars reticulata, and the thalamus. Basal ganglia output is directed toward the frontal lobe and brainstem nuclei, and is thus largely implicated in the control and selection of action.

Studies of the functional anatomy of the basal ganglia suggest that there are discrete basal ganglia regions and circuits that subserve different modes of behavioral control and action (Alexander et al. 1986; Redgrave et al. 2010). For example, the sensorimotor striatum (i.e., the putamen) receives input from the primary motor and sensory cortices, and premotor regions, which directs output to supplemental motor areas involved with the selection and initiation of overlearned movement sequences. The associative striatum (i.e., head of the caudate nucleus) receives input from dorsolateral prefrontal regions and association cortices of the parietal and temporal lobes that are associated with higher-level cognitive functions such as decision-making and goal-directed action. The ventral striatum (i.e., the nucleus accumbens) receives input from the anterior cingulate and medial orbitofrontal regions of the cortex, along with several limbic structures, and is implicated in motivated action and reward-based learning. Output from these discrete basal ganglia circuits, therefore, assist in the selection, implementation, and control of different types of action or behavior, with sensorimotor regions facilitating the selection of well-learned, habitual responses, and more associative regions facilitating the selection of goal-directed action.

In PD, degeneration of the dopamine-producing cells of the substantia nigra pars compacta leads to a loss of tonic dopaminergic input, which is required for normal function of the sensorimotor striatum (e.g., Damier et al. 1999; Kish et al. 1998; Redgrave et al. 2010). This leads to reduced efficiency and a degraded signal to noise ratio of the striatal pathways that are associated with facilitating the timely selection of automatic or habitual components of movement, including the appropriate scaling of movement amplitude and velocity (e.g., DeLong 1990; Desmurget, Grafton, Vindras, Grea, and Turner 2004). In a series of behavioral and imaging studies, Wu, Hallett, and colleagues present data suggesting that PD is associated with a specific deficit in motor automaticity characterized by a breakdown movements that rely on habitual or automatic control, whereas goal-directed action that relies more heavily on attentional networks is (relatively) preserved (e.g., Wu, Chan and Hallett 2008; 2010; Wu and Hallett 2005; Wu, Hallett, and Chan 2015; Wu, Liu, Zhang, Hallett, Zheng, and Chan 2014; Wu, Wang, Wang, Hallett, Zang, Wu, and Chan 2012). Data from several studies corroborate this interpretation, as individuals with PD often exhibit improvements in motor control when cued to increase attention and effort when performing several activities of daily living. In light of these findings, the variability in speech motor impairment reported across studies and patients may be influenced by the extent to which a speaker relies more heavily on either goal-directed or habitual control in a given speaking environment. The current paper will narrowly review changes in acoustic features of articulation associated with adopting more goal-directed speaking styles such as clear, loud, and slow speech in speakers with PD.

2 Effects of Parkinson Disease on Speech Articulation

Data from several studies indicate that speakers with PD exhibit differences in speech articulation that are consistent with a hypokinetic movement disorder. For example, studies suggest that speakers with PD exhibit reduced amplitude and velocity of lip opening and closing gestures compared to controls (e.g., Bandini et al. 2016; Darling and Huber 2011; Forrest, Weismer, and Turner 1989; Hirose, Kiritani, Ushijima, Yoshioka, and Sawashima 1981; Hunker, Abbs, and Barlow 1982). Likewise, studies measuring lingual movement in parkinsonian speech also indicate that speakers with PD exhibit smaller lingual excursions than neurologically healthy controls (e.g., Kearney, Giles, Haworth, Faloutsos, Baljko, and Yunusova 2017; Walsh and Smith 2012). Additionally, speakers exhibit changes in speech rate and pause timing. Overall, studies suggest that speakers with PD often exhibit a smaller range of articulatory movement and differences in speech motor timing compared to control speakers (e.g., Darling and Huber 2011; Forrest et al. 1989; Hunker et al. 1982; Hirose et al. 1981; Kearney et al. 2017; Walsh and Smith 2012).

2.1   Speech Timing in Habitual Parkinsonian Speech

Several measures of speech timing have been examined including voice onset time (VOT), measures of speech rate, and metrics reflecting the number, duration, and proportion of silent intervals within the speech signal including pause.

VOT. Examinations of VOT in speakers with PD appear to show little consensus, with some authors reporting shorter VOTs relative to healthy controls (Flint, Black, Campbell-Taylor, Gailey, and Levinton 1992), others reporting longer VOTs relative to healthy controls (Forrest et al. 1989), and still others reporting no difference in VOTs relative to healthy controls (Bunton and Weismer 2002; Fischer and Goberman 2010). For example, Forrest et al. (1989) compared a number of acoustic and kinematic measures of articulatory timing between individuals with PD and control speakers. The authors reported significantly longer VOTs for the voiced bilabial plosive (i.e., /b/). Though not significant, the VOTs for the voiceless bilabial plosive (i.e., /p/) were on average shorter in the PD group compared to the control group. In another study, Flint et al. (1992) suggests individuals with PD exhibit shorter voiceless VOTs compared to neurologically healthy controls.

Lieberman et al. (1992) presented a different perspective and compared the relative overlap in VOT for speakers with and without PD. Because VOT is longer for voiceless compared to voiced stop consonants, it is considered a phonological marker used for consonant identification. Lieberman et al. (1992) observed that a subgroup of 9 individuals with PD exhibited significantly more VOT overlap than the control participants. Of these nine speakers, 7 were characterized as having moderate PD, while the other 2 were characterized as mild. A recent note by Whitfield, Reif, and Goberman (2018), replicated this finding in a different sample of speakers with PD using a task designed for examining stop consonant production and VOT. Analysis revealed that speakers with PD exhibited greater overlap in the distribution of VOT values for voiced and voiceless stop consonants than age-matched control speakers that could not be explained in by differences in speaking rate between the groups (Whitfield et al. 2018). Data from these studies suggest that PD may affect the degree of temporal contrast between voiced and voiceless cognates.

Speech Rate. A number of authors have examined speaking and articulatory rate in individuals with PD (e.g., Canter 1963; Goberman, Coelho, and Robb 2005; Ludlow, Connor, and Bassich 1987; McRae, Tjaden and Schoonings 2002; Skodda and Schlegel 2008). Data from these studies suggest that individuals with PD can exhibit speaking rates that are faster (e.g., McRae et al. 2002), slower (e.g., Ludlow et al. 1987), or statistically similar (e.g., Canter 1963; Goberman et al. 2005; Rusz et al. 2011; Skodda et al. 2011a, 2011b; Tjaden and Wilding 2011) to the rates of neurologically healthy talkers. However, there is substantial variation in measurement criteria that have been used to quantify speech rate measures. Speech rate, a common measure expressed in phonemes, syllables, or words per unit time, is typically characterized as the number of constituent units (e.g., syllables) produced divided by total speaking time including both sounded and silent intervals. Articulation rate, referred to as a net speech rate by some, is calculated by dividing the number of constitute units produced by spoken interval duration, and, thus, removes the effect of pause intervals from the measurement (e.g., Goberman et al. 2005). Pauses in speech are typically defined as a silent interval bounded by sounded speech lasting longer than a specified duration. However, several thresholds have been used to operationalize articulation rate measures, with some authors defining pause as a silent interval lasting longer than 200 or 250 ms (e.g., Tjaden and Wilding 2011), while others include silent intervals below 200 ms (e.g., Goberman et al. 2005; Skodda et al. 2011a, 2011b).

Studies examining speech articulation and shorter silent intervals within speech runs (e.g., 10 to 15 ms) suggest that speakers with PD exhibit aberrant speech motor timing associated with segmental aspects of speech sound articulation (e.g., Skodda and Schlegel 2008, 2009; Whitfield and Gravelin 2019). For example, several studies suggest that speakers with PD exhibit faster rates and less consistent syllable timing during syllable diadochokinetic rate tasks (e.g., Rusz et al. 2011; Skodda and Schlegel 2008). In connected speech, speakers with PD exhibit fewer silent intervals within- and between-words (e.g., Skodda and Schlegel 2008, 2009; Whitfield and Gravelin 2019). Additionally, within- and between-word silent interval durations tend to be longer in the speech of individuals with PD compared to controls (e.g., Skodda and Schlegel 2008, 2009; Whitfield and Gravelin 2019), potentially indicating a slight delay in the transition between syllables and words. Finally, work by Skodda and colleagues also suggests that speakers with PD exhibit a greater degree of acceleration in articulation rate across a speaking task than control talkers (e.g., Skodda and Schlegel 2008).

Authors who have restricted pause to longer silent interval durations (e.g., 200 to 250 ms) to more clearly differentiate articulatory from prosodic events report that speakers with PD exhibit prosodic deficits associated with aberrant speech and pause timing (e.g., Goberman et al. 2005; Solomon and Hixon 1993; Tjaden and Wilding 2011). For example, Hammen and Yorkston (1996) reported that speakers with PD exhibited shorter speaking durations and longer pause durations than controls. Solomon and Hixon (1993) reported that speakers with PD exhibited shorter inter-pause speech rates, though the duration of inspiratory breaths between speech runs were similar to controls. Tjaden and Wilding (2011) and Goberman et al. (2005) reported that speakers with PD exhibit a lower speech-to-pause ratio that control talkers, indicating than parkinsonian speech exhibited proportionally more pause than the speech of healthy controls.

Several studies seem to indicate that speakers with PD exhibit a greater portion of pause at locations that do not align with major syntactic boundaries of the spoken utterance (e.g., Hammen and Yorkston 1996; Huber, Darling, Francis, and Zhang 2012; Tjaden and Wilding 2011; Whitfield and Gravelin 2019). For example, Huber et al. (2012) reported that speakers with PD exhibited a higher frequency of inspiratory breaths at syntactically inappropriate boundaries than control speakers. In a report by Tjaden and Wilding (2011), speakers with PD exhibited a slightly lower proportion of grammatically appropriate pauses during a habitual reading task, a trend that approached statistical significance. During slower than normal speech, however, controls exhibited a decrease in the proportion of pauses at syntactically inappropriate boundaries such that there were no differences between speakers with PD and controls for the slow speaking rate. To date, judgements of the appropriateness of pause locations within connected speech have relied heavily on conventions of written syntax (e.g., Hammen and Yorkston 1996; Huber et al. 2012; Tjaden and Wilding 2011; Whitfield and Gravelin 2019). Substantial evidence suggests, however, that written syntactical structures do not directly map onto spoken language and prosody. Therefore, future work should aim to more directly address speech prosody using a framework that better accounts for the structure of spoken language.

Different conclusions reported across multiple studies may suggest that speakers with PD exhibit greater than normal intra- and inter-speaker variation. However, methodological differences in speech and pause measurement make direct comparison to the results from prior studies challenging. Closer examination shows that while speakers with PD may not exhibit different speech or articulation rates than controls (e.g., Goberman et al. 2005; Skodda et al. 2011a, 2011b; Tjaden and Wilding 2011; Whitfield and Gravelin 2019), they do exhibit a greater proportion of pause time between speech runs (e.g., Goberman et al. 2005; Hammen and Yorkston 1996; Tjaden and Wilding, 2011) and shorter speech runs that contain shorter and less frequent silent intervals than controls speakers (Skodda et al. 2011a; Solomon and Hixon 1993; Whitfield and Gravelin 2019). Overall, these data along with the findings from studies of VOT suggest the hypokinetic movement disorder associated with PD affects speech motor timing. The physiological processes underlying deficits in speech and pause timing have been hypothesized to relate to the untimely selection of speech motor programs that lead to disruptions in speech fluency (e.g., Civier, Bullock, Max, and Guenther 2013; Whitfield, Delong, Goberman, and Blomgren 2018) and difficulty coordinating the dynamic aspects between the respiratory, phonatory, and articulatory subsystems (e.g. Huber et al. 2012; Solomon and Hixon 1993).

2.2   Formant Space in Habitual Parkinsonian Speech

In addition to differences in speech timing, hypokinetic changes in articulatory kine-matics associated with PD spectrally map onto formant frequency patterns. A formant is a measured resonance of the vocal tract (e.g., Kent and Vorperian 2018; Titze et al. 2015), and during vowel-like productions reflects the size and shape of the vocal tract cavities. The first and second formant frequencies (F1 and F2) are strongly coupled to the location and degree of constriction of the vocal tract, as well as the lip configuration (e.g., Stevens and House 1956; Story, Title, and Hoffman 1998). Perceptually, F1 and F2 are strongly linked to vowel identity (e.g., Hillenbrand, Getty, Clark, and Wheeler 1995; Peterson and Barney 1952).

Several derived formant frequency measures have been used to characterize for-mant space. Perhaps the most widely used family of formant frequency measures are the point-based vowel space area metrics, which typically utilize formant pairs (F1, F2) extracted from segments of target vowel intervals to construct a two-dimensional area in formant space. These are more global acoustic metrics of formant space that are calculated from formant frequency pairs (F1, F2) of specified vowels within target words embedded a carrier phrase (e.g., Rusz et al. 2011), sentences (e.g., Lam and Tjaden 2016), a reading passage (e.g., McRae et al. 2002; Tjaden and Wilding 2004), or extemporaneous speech. The most commonly used vowel space area variants include the triangular and quadrilateral vowel space area, calculated from the formant pairs extracted from the mid-point or steady state of the "corner" vowels /i/, /a/, and /u/ and /i/, /a/, /u/, and /æ/ vowels respectively. Other point-based vowel space metrics include formant frequency ratios such as the Formant Centralization Ratio (FCR; Sapir et al. 2010) and its reciprocal the Vowel Articulation Index (VAI; Roy, Nissen, Dromey, and Sapir 2009; Skodda et al. 2011 2012), which are ratios of F1 and F2 values extracted from /i/, /a/, and /u/ that reflect formant centralization and expansion, respectively. In addition to global measures of formant space, authors have also attempted to capture more dynamic aspects of formant change associated with intravocalic movement. Such metrics include the range and rate of change of formant frequency movement during diphthong vowels, as well as other metrics of intravocalic change in monophthong vowels.

Other authors have proposed vowel space metrics that are based on distributional characteristics of formant frequency traces, rather than a few isolated points in formant space (e.g., Sandoval, Berisha, Utianski, Liss, and Spanias 2013; Story and Bunton 2017; Whitfield and Goberman 2014, 2017a). For these approaches, authors sample formant frequency trajectories of the voiced portion of connected speech utterances to form a data distribution in F1, F2 space. Example metrics include the vowel space hull area (e.g., Hsu, Jiao, McAuliffe, Berisha, Wu, and Levy 2017; Sandoval et al. 2013) that is based on the perimeter of the formant frequency data cloud, the articulatory-acoustic vowel space (AAVS; e.g., Whitfield and Goberman 2014; Whitfield and Mehta 2019) that is based on the variance of the F1, F2 data distribution, and vowel space density metrics (VSD; e.g., Story and Bunton 2017; Whitfield and Mehta 2019) that are based on the area of formant space at or above a specified threshold of the formant density distribution. Others have examined metrics such as the coefficient of variation or interquartile range of F2 to capture formant frequency variation associated with connected speech (e.g., Kuo and Tjaden 2016).

Because speakers with PD exhibit a reduction in articulatory movement compared to healthy controls, measures of formant space are often smaller for speakers with PD than for healthy speakers (e.g., Bang, Min, Sohn, and Cho 2013; Hsu et al. 2017; Kang, Yoon, Lee, and Seong 2010; Kuo and Tjaden 2016; Rusz et al. 2013; Sapir, Ramig, Spielman, and Fox, 2011; Skodda et al. 2011b, 2012; Tjaden, Lam, and Wilding 2013; Watson and Munson 2008; Whitfield and Goberman 2014). For example, Tjaden et al. (2013) observed that speakers with PD exhibited smaller quadrilateral vowel space area calculated from corner vowels of target words using habitual speech, compared to healthy controls. Likewise, speakers with PD exhibit formant ratios that are consistent with greater formant centralization than healthy control speakers (e.g., Sapir et al. 2010; Skodda et al. 2011b).

Other studies of working vowel space metrics that quantify the variation in the distribution of formant frequency trajectories have also found that speakers with PD exhibit a reduction in formant space compared to controls (e.g., Hsu et al. 2017; Kuo and Tjaden 2016; Whitfield and Goberman 2014, Whitfield and Mehta 2019). For example, Whitfield and Goberman (2014) reported that speakers with PD exhibited significantly smaller AAVS values than controls for formant frequency traces extracted from the first sentence of the Rainbow passage. Additionally, listeners reliably reported lower ratings of speech clarity for the speakers with PD than controls (Whitfield and Goberman 2014). Hsu et al. (2017) reported that Mandarin speakers with PD exhibited smaller vowel space hull areas calculated from formant frequency traces of a reading passage than control speakers. In another recent study, Whitfield and Mehta (2019) found that the area associated with the greatest concentration of formant data (i.e., VSD_{90}) was significantly smaller for speakers with PD compared to controls, indicating a greater degree of formant centralization.

Despite the relatively common finding that speakers with PD exhibit a smaller formant space than controls, data from a handful of studies suggest that differences in habitual vowel space between speakers with PD and controls are not statistically significant (e.g., Rusz et al. 2011; Sapir et al. 2007, 2010; Tjaden and Wilding 2004; Weismer et al. 2001). For example, Weismer et al. (2001) reported statistically similar values between speakers with PD and controls for triangular vowel space area computed from selected corner vowels of sentence stimuli. Similarly, Rusz et al. (2011) reported no significant differences in triangular vowel space area between speakers with and without PD for extracted isolated vowels. In another study, Whitfield and Mehta (2019) did not observe differences in the habitual AAVS or vowel space hull area between speakers with PD and healthy controls, although speakers with PD did exhibit significantly smaller AAVS than controls when using a clear speech style.

Several factors may explain why some authors have not observed the expected differences in formant space between speakers with PD and healthy controls. First, data from several investigations suggest that traditional point-based vowel space metrics, such as triangular and quadrilateral vowel space area may not be sensitive to subtle differences in vowel articulation between speakers with PD and controls because of high intra-speaker variation and an undersampling of acoustic data (e.g., Sandoval et al. 2013; Sapir et al. 2010; Rusz et al. 2013; Whitfield and Goberman 2014, 2017a). As such, several authors have explored more sensitive formant space metrics such as normalized formant ratios and measures of working formant space that characterize the full formant frequency distribution of connected speech utterances (e.g., Sandoval et al. 2013; Sapir et al. 2010; Whitfield and Goberman 2014, 2017a; Whitfield and Mehta 2019). Additionally, data from several studies suggests that the speaking task used to elicit vowel productions affects measures of formant space. For example, Rusz et al. (2013) reported significant differences in vowel space area and VAI between speakers with PD and controls for vowel space metrics measured from sentence reading and monologue production, whereas there were no group differences for metrics extracted from a sustained phonation task. These data suggest that more naturalistic speech tasks, such as reading or monologue data, may improve the diagnostic sensitivity of articulatory dysfunction in PD (Rusz et al. 2013). Still other authors have suggested that speakers with PD may exhibit improved speech production during explicit measurement of voice and speech as compared to truly habitual, conversational speech (Bunton and Keintz 2008; Goberman and Elmer 2005).

3 Speech Style Modulation: Clear, Loud, and Slow Speech

Several authors have documented the extent to which speakers with PD exhibit expected changes in speech production when adopting modulating speech production to higher effort speaking styles such as clear, loud, and slow speech (e.g., Goberman, and Elmer 2005; Kearney et al. 2017; Lam and Tjaden 2016; Mefferd 2017; Tjaden et al. 2013; Tjaden, Sussman, and Wilding 2014; Tjaden and Wilding 2004; Whitfield and Goberman, 2014; Whitfield and Mehta 2019). Studies of speech style modulation demonstrate that when healthy talkers are instructed to speak louder, clearer, or slower than usual, speakers exhibit changes in speech production that optimize acoustic features that improve the intelligibility of the spoken utterance (e.g., Picheny, Durlach, and Braida 1986; Lam, Tjaden, and Wilding 2012). Changes in speech production associated with clear speech include an increase in speech intensity and a reduction in speech rate (e.g., Krause and Braida 2002; 2004; Picheny et al. 1986; Lam et al. 2012). Rate reduction can be achieved by a combination of strategies including, increasing pause length, increasing segment durations, decreasing movement velocity, increasing range of motion, or decreasing coarticulatory overlap between articulatory gestures (e.g., Adams, Weismer, and Kent 1993). Additionally, clear speech is associated with an increase in vowel distinctiveness that is associated with an increase articulatory range of motion and expansion of formant space (e.g., Krause and Braida 2004; Lam and Tjaden 2016; Picheny et al. 1986; Whitfield and Goberman 2017a). Findings from prior studies suggest that these changes cannot be solely explained by changes in speaking rate, and are, therefore, a distinct characteristic of these higher effort, clear speech styles (e.g., Krause and Braida 2002).

3.1 Speech Style Modulation in Speakers with Parkinson Disease

Overall, data from several studies suggest that speakers with PD exhibit the expected changes in speech articulation when utilizing clearer and louder speaking styles (e.g., Darling and Huber 2011; Dromey, Ramig, and Johnson 1995; Goberman and Elmer 2005; Gravelin and Whitfield 2019; Kearney et al. 2017; Lam and Tjaden 2013; McRae et al. 2002; Mefferd 2017; Neel 2009; Tjaden and Martel-Sauvageau 2017; Tjaden et al. 2013, 2014; Tjaden and Wilding 2005; Whitfield and Goberman 2014; Whitfield and Mehta 2019). For example, Tjaden and colleagues have conducted several studies on the extent to which the instructions to speaker slower, louder, and clearer than usual affect acoustic measures of articulation in parkinsonian speakers (e.g., Lam and Tjaden 2013; Tjaden and Martel-Sauvageau 2017; Tjaden and Wilding 2004; Tjaden et al. 2013, 2014). Data from these studies suggest that cues to speak slower than usual yield the largest reductions in speaking rate, cues to speak louder than usual yield the largest increases in speech intensity, cues to clearer than usual lead to the largest increases in measures of formant space (e.g., Lam and Tjaden 2013; Tjaden and Martel-Sauvageau 2017; Tjaden and Wilding 2004; Tjaden et al., 2013, 2014). However, speaking slower or louder than usual may also lead to increases in formant space (e.g., Tjaden et al. 2013; Tjaden and Wilding 2004) and cues to speak clearer than usual also lead to reductions in speaking rate and increases in speech intensity (e.g., Lam and Tjaden 2013; Tjaden and Martel-Sauvageau 2017; Tjaden et al. 2013, 2014; Whitfield, Dromey, and Palmer 2018; Whitfield and Mehta 2019).

Studies of formant space suggest speakers with PD generally exhibit the expected increase in vowel space metrics when adopting a clearer speaking style (e.g., Lam and Tjaden 2016; Tjaden et al. 2013). This finding is typically observed for both vowel space area metrics based on isolated points in formant space (e.g., Lam and Tjaden 2016; Tjaden et al. 2013), as well as working vowel space measures based on continuously extracted trajectories in connected speech (Whitfield and Goberman 2014;

Whitfield and Mehta 2019). For example, in a study of several measures of working vowel space extracted from a reading passage, Whitfield and Mehta (2019) reported significant increases in the AAVS, vowel space hull area, and vowel space density when speakers with and without PD were instructed to speak more clearly than usual. Therefore, several studies document that speakers with PD exhibit significant increases in formant space when instructed to speak in a manner that is clearer than the habitual mode of speech motor control.

Of note, however, some studies have reported that speakers with PD exhibit a lesser degree of clarity-related increase in vowel space area than expected for healthy controls (e.g., Goberman and Elmer 2005; Whitfield and Mehta 2019). For example, Goberman and Elmer (2005) reported that a group of speakers with PD did not exhibit the expected increases in traditional vowel space area measured from the midpoint of corner vowels embedded within a carrier phrase when using a clearer than usual style. In another study, Whitfield and Mehta (2019) observed significant clarity-related increases in traditional vowel space area measured in a comparable speaking task. However, clarity-related increases in working formant space (i.e., AAVS & VSD_{10}) of a reading passage were significantly less than the increase observed for neurologically healthy controls between habitual and clear speech styles. Thus, data suggest that the clear speech response observed in formant space metrics may be less robust or more variable in speakers with PD compared to healthy controls (e.g., Goberman and Elmer 2005; Whitfield and Mehta 2019).

In addition to changes in the spectral characteristics of vowels, reports suggest that speakers with PD also exhibit expected changes in speech timing when adopting more effortful speaking styles, such as clear, loud and slow speech. Data from Tjaden and colleagues suggest that instructions to speak slower leads to greater rate reductions than instructions for clearer or louder speech (e.g., Tjaden et al. 2013; Tjaden and Wilding 2004). However, speakers with PD exhibit reductions in speaking rate (e.g., Lam and Tjaden 2016) and increases in pause durations (Gravelin and Whitfield 2019) when instructed to speak clearly or overenunciate. For example, Lam and Tjaden (2016) reported that clear speech styles were associated with longer vowel and consonant segment durations and slower articulation rates than habitual speech. Tjaden and Martel-Sauvageau (2017) reported a significant group by condition interaction for articulation rate. Visual inspection of the mean data and post hoc comparisons revealed that while speakers with PD exhibited a reduction in articulation rate from habitual to clear speech style, they exhibited a faster articulation rate than controls for the clear speech style, but not the habitual style. Similarly, data from Gravelin and Whitfield (2019) revealed that both speakers with and without PD exhibited a significant increase in pause durations at syntactic boundaries, whereas only control speakers exhibited increases in short within- and between-word silent interval durations associated with articulatory events. Because speakers with PD exhibit longer silent interval durations in the habitual style than controls, speakers with PD exhibited only slight increases in short within- and between-word interval durations between habitual and clear speech (Gravelin and Whitfield 2019; Whitfield and Gravelin 2019). Therefore, while there is clear evidence that speakers with PD make adjustments to the speech production system when instructed to speak clearer or louder than usual, data from several studies suggest that speakers with PD may exhibit a clear speech response that is less robust or more variable than the clear speech response of neurologically healthy controls.

4 Summary and Conclusions

In summary, comparison of results across multiple studies examining acoustic measures of articulation produced using habitual and clear speech styles suggests that speakers with PD tend to exhibit differences in habitual articulation rate and formant space from healthy control speakers. Articulatory-acoustic changes associated with PD are consistent with hypokinetic motor symptoms, including a rushed or accelerating articulation with breakdowns in speech fluency that occupies a smaller region of formant space (e.g., Hsu et al. 2017; Whitfield and Goberman 2014, Whitfield and Mehta 2019). Additionally, speakers with PD exhibit the expected reduction in speaking rate and expansion of formant space when instructed to de-automatize speech production by speaking clearer, louder, or slower than usual (e.g., Sapir 2014; Lam and Tjaden 2016; Tjaden et al. 2013; Whitfield and Goberman 2014, Whitfield and Mehta 2019). A handful of reports, however, document no differences in habitual articulation rates and formant space metrics between speakers with and without PD (e.g., Sapir et al. 2007; Weismer et al. 2001; Whitfield and Mehta 2019). Additionally, some authors have observed less robust changes to speech articulation between habitual and clear speech styles in speakers with PD compared to controls (e.g., Goberman and Elmer 2005; Gravelin and Whitfield 2019; Tjaden and Martel-Sauvageau 2017; Whitfield and Mehta 2019).

While several factors may contribute to the different trends observed between studies, one potential factor that may account for variation within and between speakers with PD is the extent to which a spoken utterance relies on more automatic or goal-directed control processes. Neurophysiological and behavioral data suggest that habitual motor control in individuals with PD relies more heavily on goal-directed, cognitive resources (e.g., Redgrave et al. 2010; Wu et al. 2014, 2015). Several studies report that individuals with PD exhibit impaired motor automaticity characterized by greater susceptibility to motor control interference from concurrent task demands that is observed for even simple, well-established motor patterns (e.g., Ho, Iansek, and Bradshaw 2002; Plummer-D'Amato, Altmann, and Reilly 2011; O'Shea, Morris, and Iansek 2002; Wu and Hallett 2005; Wu et al. 2014). Additionally, individuals with PD exhibit impairments in the later stages of motor learning when performance of a newly acquired skill is automated (e.g., Wu and Hallett 2005; Whitfield and Goberman 2017b). Neuroimaging data corroborate these findings, demonstrating that individuals with PD exhibit significantly greater activation of the dorsolateral prefrontal networks when performing simple motor tasks than neurologically healthy controls, where activation levels are largely confined to the primary sensorimotor cortex. Taken together, data from these studies suggest that successful performance of a motor task in the parkinsonian state requires the engagement of goal-directed, attentional networks, thus, bypassing the dysfunctional habit control system (e.g., Redgrave et al. 2010; Wu et al. 2015).

Prior authors have postulated that that speakers with PD may compensate for speech production deficits by independently initiating clear speech strategies even during a speech production task where no explicit clarity instruction is given (e.g., Goberman and Elmer 2005). Other data support the notion that isolated speech tasks that require little-to-no attentional load such as word reading, sentence or paragraph reading, and even short extemporaneous samples yield clearer and louder speech acoustics and improved intelligibility than conversational speech recorded during an interview (e.g., Bunton and Keintz 2008). It is, therefore, possible that speakers with PD exhibit performance effects that may shift control toward a more goal-directed mode of speech motor control that is clearer and less impaired than habitual speech produced in everyday communication environments that include multiple, competing demands.

This hypothesis could account for circumstances where a speaker with PD produces speech samples that exhibit similar acoustic features to control speakers, but report or exhibit speech production deficits in other environments or situations. As reviewed above, there are instances where no significant differences between speakers with and without PD are observed for a variety of acoustic measures of articulation including speech rate and vowel space area (e.g., Sapir et al. 2007; Rusz et al. 2011; Weismer et al. 2001; Whitfield and Mehta 2019). Additionally, several studies demonstrate that performance of a secondary distractor task affects speakers with PD differently than healthy controls (e.g., Ho et al. 2002; Holmes et al. 2010; Plummer-D'Amato et al. 2011; O'Shea et al. 2002; Whitfield and Goberman 2017b; Whitfield et al. 2019). For example, data suggest that low demand secondary motor tasks, such as turning a nut and bolt or making continuous circling motions may impact speech acoustics, especially for extemporaneous speech tasks. Whitfield et al. (2019), however, reported little to no effect of continuous circling motions on speech acoustics of a reading task, suggesting that the dual-task effect may not be as robust for some individuals, especially for secondary tasks that require little-to-no attentional resources. Data from other studies, however, show a more reliable and robust dual-task degradation effect on speech acoustics for secondary task that require more attentional resources. For example, several authors have reported that speakers with PD exhibit greater changes in speech acoustics when performing attention-demanding visuomotor tasks than control speakers (e.g., Ho et al. 2002; Whitfield and Goberman 2017b). Overall, greater changes in speech production that are observed when speakers with PD perform a secondary task suggest that the basic act of speaking in PD requires a greater degree of attentional resources than in healthy control talkers.

Likewise, this hypothesis could account for instances where a speaker or group of speakers with PD exhibit a less robust clear speech response than expected. As reviewed, there are instances in the literature where speakers with PD exhibit a change in speech acoustics between habitual and clear speech that is non-significant (e.g., Goberman and Elmer 2005) or significantly less than the clear speech benefit observed in neurologically healthy controls (e.g., Gravelin and Whitfield 2019; Tjaden and Martel-Sauvageau 2017; Whitfield and Mehta 2019). In light of the abovementioned hypothesis, habitual speech may rely more heavily on goal-directed control. A ceiling effect would account for the reduced clear speech response observed in these studies, as the habitual sample produced by some speakers with PD may have been produced with a clearer-than-habitual production.

In light of this hypothesis, there is a critical need to develop standardized speech collection protocols that elicit speech samples in a variety speech tasks, styles, and conditions to capture the full degree of intraspeaker variation in parkinsonian speech. Several factors appear to affect acoustic measures of speech articulation in both speakers with and without PD. Connected speech production tasks such as reading, extemporaneous or monologue production, and conversation may elicit speech samples that are more ecologically valid, providing a better representation of speech production. Additionally, authors have explored the extent to which performance of a secondary task interferes with speech production, as dual-task performance relies more heavily on attentional, goal-directed processes that are limited in capacity (e.g., Bunton and Keintz 2008; Whitfield et al. 2019; Whitfield and Goberman 2017b). Therefore, examining speech under more attention-demanding conditions that tax the goal-directed system may reveal the extent to which speakers direct attentional resources toward articulating clearly even during habitual speech. In all, the literature suggests that there is a wide range of intra- and inter-speaker variability in Parkinson disease. Gaining a deeper understanding of what factors account for this variability will enhance models and systems aimed at characterizing parkinsonian speech for diagnostic and rehabilitation purposes.

References

Hirtz, D., Thurman, D.J., Gwinn-Hardy, K., Mohamed, M., Chaudhuri, A.R., Zalutsky, R.: How common are the "common" neurologic disorders? Neurology **68**(5), 326–337 (2007)

De Lau, L.M., Breteler, M.M.: Epidemiology of Parkinson's disease. Lancet Neurol. **5**(6), 525–535 (2006)

Wirdefeldt, K., Adami, H.O., Cole, P., Trichopoulos, D., Mandel, J.: Epidemiology and etiology of Parkinson's disease: a review of the evidence. Euro. J. Epidemiol. **26**(1), 1 (2011)

Dickson, D.W., et al.: Evidence that incidental Lewy body disease is pre-symptomatic Parkinson's disease. Acta Neuropathol. **115**(4), 437–444 (2008)

Fearnley, J.M., Lees, A.J.: Ageing and Parkinson's disease: substantia nigra regional selectivity. Brain **114**(5), 2283–2301 (1991)

Lang, A.E., Lozano, A.M.: Parkinson's disease. N. Engl. J. Med. **339**(16), 1130–1143 (1998)

Rabey, J.M., Burns, R.S.: Neurochemistry. In: S.A., Factor, W.J. Weiner (Eds.) Parkinson's disease: Diagnosis and clinical management, Second edition, New York, NY: Demos, pp. 227–243 (2008)

Rodriguez-Oroz, M.C., et al.: Initial clinical manifestations of Parkinson's disease: features and pathophysiological mechanisms. Lancet Neurol. **8**(12), 1128–1139 (2009)

Damier, P., Hirsch, E.C., Agid, Y., Graybiel, A.M.: The substantia nigra of the human brain II Patterns of loss of dopamine-containing neurons in Parkinson's disease. Brain **122**(8), 1437–1448 (1999)

Kish, S.J., Shannak, K., Rajput, A., Deck, J.H., Hornykiewicz, O.: Aging produces a specific pattern of striatal dopamine loss: implications: for the etiology of idiopathic Parkinson's disease. J. Neurochem. **58**(2), 642–648 (1992)

Redgrave, P., et al.: Goal-directed and habitual control in the basal ganglia: implications for Parkinson's disease. Nat. Rev. Neurosci. **11**(11), 760 (2010)

Wu, T., et al.: Basal ganglia circuits changes in Parkinson's disease patients. Neurosci. Lett. **524** (1), 55–59 (2012)

Braak, H., Ghebremedhin, E., Rüb, U., Bratzke, H., Del Tredici, K.: Stages in the development of Parkinson's disease-related pathology. Cell Tissue Res. **318**(1), 121–134 (2004)

Darley, F.L., Aronson, A.E., Brown, J.R.: Clusters of deviant speech dimensions in the dysarthrias. J. Speech Hear. Res. **12**(3), 462–496 (1969a)

Darley, F.L., Aronson, A.E., Brown, J.R.: Differential diagnostic patterns of dysarthria. J. Speech Hear. Res. **12**(2), 246–269 (1969b)

Ho, A.K., Iansek, R., Marigliani, C., Bradshaw, J.L., Gates, S.: Speech impairment in a large sample of patients with Parkinson's disease. Behav. Neurol. **11**(3), 131–137 (1999)

Logemann, J.A., Fisher, H.B., Boshes, B., Blonsky, E.R.: Frequency and cooccurrence of vocal tract dysfunctions in the speech of a large sample of Parkinson patients. J. Speech Hear. Disord. **43**(1), 47–57 (1978)

Sapir, S.: Multiple factors are involved in the dysarthria associated with Parkinson's disease: a review with implications for clinical practice and research. J. Speech Lang. Hear. Res. **57**(4), 1330–1343 (2014)

Galaz, Z., et al.: Degree of Parkinson's disease severity estimation based on speech signal processing. In: 2016 39th International Conference on Telecommunications and Signal Processing (TSP), pp. 503–506. IEEE (2016)

Tsanas, A., Little, M.A., McSharry, P.E., Spielman, J., Ramig, L.O.: Novel speech signal processing algorithms for high-accuracy classification of Parkinson's disease. IEEE Trans. Biomed. Eng. **59**(5), 1264–1271 (2012)

Vásquez-Correa, J.C., et al.: Convolutional neural networks and a transfer learning strategy to classify Parkinson's disease from speech in three different languages. In: Iberoamerican Congress on Pattern Recognition, pp. 697–706. Springer, Cham (2019). https://doi.org/10. 1007/978-3-030-33904-3_66

Alexander, G.E., DeLong, M.R., Strick, P.L.: Parallel organization of functionally segregated circuits linking basal ganglia and cortex. Ann. Rev. Neurosci. **9**(1), 357–381 (1986)

DeLong, M.R.: Primate models of movement disorders of basal ganglia origin. Trends Neurosci. **13**(7), 281–285 (1990)

Desmurget, M., Grafton, S.T., Vindras, P., Grea, H., Turner, R.S.: The basal ganglia network mediates the planning of movement amplitude. Eur. J. Neurosci. **19**(10), 2871–2880 (2004)

Wu, T., Chan, P., Hallett, M.: Modifications of the interactions in the motor networks when a movement becomes automatic. J. Physiol. **586**(17), 4295–4304 (2008)

Wu, T., Chan, P., Hallett, M.: Effective connectivity of neural networks in automatic movements in Parkinson's disease. Neuroimage **49**(3), 2581–2587 (2010)

Wu, T., Hallett, M.: A functional MRI study of automatic movements in patients with Parkinson's disease. Brain **128**(10), 2250–2259 (2005)

Wu, T., Hallett, M., Chan, P.: Motor automaticity in Parkinson's disease. Neurobiol. Dis. **82**, 226–234 (2015)

Wu, T., Liu, J., Zhang, H., Hallett, M., Zheng, Z., Chan, P.: Attention to automatic movements in Parkinson's disease: modified automatic mode in the striatum. Cereb. Cortex **25**(10), 3330–3342 (2014)

Bandini, A., et al.: Markerless analysis of articulatory movements in patients with Parkinson's disease. J. Voice **30**(6), 766-e1 (2016)

Darling, M., Huber, J.E.: Changes to articulatory kinematics in response to loudness cues in individuals with Parkinson's disease. J. Speech Lang. Hear. Res. **54**(5), 1247–1259 (2011)

Forrest, K., Weismer, G., Turner, G.S.: Kinematic, acoustic, and perceptual analyses of connected speech produced by Parkinsonian and normal geriatric adults. J. Acoust. Soc. Am. **85**(6), 2608–2622 (1989)

Hirose, H., Kiritani, S., Ushijima, T., Yoshioka, H., Sawashima, M.: Patterns of dysarthric movements in patients with Parkinsonism. Folia Phoniatr. **33**(4), 204–215 (1981)

Hunker, C.J., Abbs, J.H., Barlow, S.M.: The relationship between parkinsonian rigidity and hypokinesia in the orofacial system: a quantitative analysis. Neurology **32**(7), 749 (1982)

Kearney, E., Giles, R., Haworth, B., Faloutsos, P., Baljko, M., Yunusova, Y.: Sentence-level movements in Parkinson's disease: loud, clear, and slow speech. J. Speech Lang. Hear. Res. **60**(12), 3426–3440 (2017)

Walsh, B., Smith, A.: Basic parameters of articulatory movements and acoustics in individuals with Parkinson's disease. Mov. Disord. **27**(7), 843–850 (2012)

Flint, A.J., Black, S.E., Campbell-Taylor, I., Gailey, G.F., Levinton, C.: Acoustic analysis in the differentiation of Parkinson's disease and major depression. J. Psycholinguist. Res. **21**(5), 383–399 (1992)

Bunton, K., Weismer, G.: Segmental level analysis of laryngeal function in persons with motor speech disorders. Folia Phoniatr. Logopaedica **54**(5), 223–239 (2002)

Fischer, E., Goberman, A.M.: Voice onset time in Parkinson disease. J. Commun. Disord. **43**(1), 21–34 (2010)

Lieberman, P., Kako, E., Friedman, J., Tajchman, G., Feldman, L.S., Jiminez, E.B.: Speech production, syntax comprehension, and cognitive deficits in Parkinson's disease. Brain Lang. **43**(2), 169–189 (1992)

Whitfield, J.A., Reif, A., Goberman, A.M.: Voicing contrast of stop consonant production in the speech of individuals with Parkinson disease ON and OFF dopaminergic medication. Clin. Linguist. Phonetics **32**(7), 587–594 (2018a)

Canter, G.J.: Speech characteristics of patients with Parkinson's disease I Intensity, pitch, and duration. J. Speech Hear. Disord. **28**(3), 221–229 (1963)

Goberman, A.M., Coelho, C.A., Robb, M.P.: Prosodic characteristics of Parkinsonian speech: the effect of levodopa-based medication. J. Med. Speech-Lang. Pathol. **13**(1), 51–69 (2005)

Ludlow, C.L., Connor, N.P., Bassich, C.J.: Speech timing in Parkinson's and Huntington's disease. Brain Lang. **32**(2), 195–214 (1987)

McRae, P.A., Tjaden, K., Schoonings, B.: Acoustic and perceptual consequences of articulatory rate change in Parkinson disease. J. Speech Lang. Hear. Res. **45**(1), 35–50 (2002)

Skodda, S., Schlegel, U.: Speech rate and rhythm in Parkinson's disease. Mov. Disord. **23**(7), 985–992 (2008)

Rusz, J., Cmejla, R., Ruzickova, H., Ruzicka, E.: Quantitative acoustic measurements for characterization of speech and voice disorders in early untreated Parkinson's disease. J. Acoust. Soc. Am. **129**(1), 350–367 (2011)

Skodda, S., Visser, W., Schlegel, U.: Gender-related patterns of dysprosody in Parkinson disease and correlation between speech variables and motor symptoms. J. Voice **25**(1), 76–82 (2011a)

Skodda, S., Visser, W., Schlegel, U.: Vowel articulation in Parkinson's disease. J. Voice **25**(4), 467–472 (2011b)

Tjaden, K., Wilding, G.: Speech and pause characteristics associated with voluntary rate reduction in Parkinson's disease and multiple sclerosis. J. Commun. Disord. **44**(6), 655–665 (2011)

Skodda, S., Rinsche, H., Schlegel, U.: Progression of dysprosody in Parkinson's disease over time—a longitudinal study. Mov. Disord. **24**(5), 716–722 (2009)

Whitfield, J.A., Gravelin, A.C.: Characterizing the distribution of silent intervals in the connected speech of individuals with Parkinson disease. J. Commun. Disord. **78**, 18–32 (2019)

Hammen, V.L., Yorkston, K.M.: Speech and pause characteristics following speech rate reduction in hypokinetic dysarthria. J. Commun. Disord. **29**(6), 429–445 (1996)

Solomon, N.P., Hixon, T.J.: Speech breathing in Parkinson's disease. J. Speech Lang. Hear. Res. **36**(2), 294–310 (1993)

Huber, J.E., Darling, M., Francis, E.J., Zhang, D.: Impact of typical aging and Parkinson's disease on the relationship among breath pausing, syntax, and punctuation. Am. J. Speech-Lang. Pathol. **21**(4), 368–379 (2012)

Civier, O., Bullock, D., Max, L., Guenther, F.H.: Computational modeling of stuttering caused by impairments in a basal ganglia thalamo-cortical circuit involved in syllable selection and initiation. Brain Lang. **126**(3), 263–278 (2013)

Whitfield, J.A., Delong, C., Goberman, A.M., Blomgren, M.: Fluency adaptation in speakers with Parkinson disease: a motor learning perspective. Int. J. Speech-Lang. Pathol. **20**(7), 699–707 (2018b)

Kent, R.D., Vorperian, H.K.: Static measurements of vowel formant frequencies and bandwidths: a review. J. Commun. Disord. **74**, 74–97 (2018)

Titze, I.R., et al.: Toward a consensus on symbolic notation of harmonics, resonances, and formants in vocalization. J Acoust. Soc. Am. **137**(5), 3005–3007 (2015)

Stevens, K.N., House, A.S.: Studies of formant transitions using a vocal tract analog. J. Acoust. Soc. Am. **28**(4), 578–585 (1956)

Story, B.H., Titze, I.R., Hoffman, E.A.: Vocal tract area functions for an adult female speaker based on volumetric imaging. J. Acoust. Soc. Am. **104**(1), 471–487 (1998)

Hillenbrand, J., Getty, L.A., Clark, M.J., Wheeler, K.: Acoustic characteristics of American English vowels. J. Acoust. Soc. Am. **97**(5), 3099–3111 (1995)

Peterson, G.E., Barney, H.L.: Control methods used in a study of the vowels. J. Acoust. Soc. Am. **24**(2), 175–184 (1952)

Lam, J., Tjaden, K.: Clear speech variants: an acoustic study in Parkinson's disease. J. Speech, Lang. Hear. Res. **59**(4), 631–646 (2016)

Tjaden, K., Wilding, G.E.: Rate and loudness manipulations in dysarthria. J. Speech Lang. Hear. Res. **47**(4), 766–783 (2004)

Sapir, S., Ramig, L.O., Spielman, J.L., Fox, C.: Formant centralization ratio: a proposal for a new acoustic measure of dysarthric speech. J. Speech Lang. Hear. Res. **53**(1), 114–125 (2010)

Roy, N., Nissen, S.L., Dromey, C., Sapir, S.: Articulatory changes in muscle tension dysphonia: evidence of vowel space expansion following manual circumlaryngeal therapy. J. Commun. Disord. **42**(2), 124–135 (2009)

Skodda, S., Grönheit, W., Schlegel, U.: Impairment of vowel articulation as a possible marker of disease progression in Parkinson's disease. PLoS ONE **7**(2), e32132 (2012)

Sandoval, S., Berisha, V., Utianski, R.L., Liss, J.M., Spanias, A.: Automatic assessment of vowel space area. J. Acoust. Soc. Am. **134**(5), EL477–EL483 (2013)

Story, B.H., Bunton, K.: Vowel space density as an indicator of speech performance. J. Acoust. Soc. Am. **141**(5), EL458–EL464 (2017)

Whitfield, J.A., Goberman, A.M.: Articulatory–acoustic vowel space: application to clear speech in individuals with Parkinson's disease. J. Commun. Disord. **51**, 19–28 (2014)

Whitfield, J.A., Goberman, A.M.: Articulatory-acoustic vowel space: associations between acoustic and perceptual measures of clear speech. Int. J. Speech-Lang. Pathol. **19**(2), 184–194 (2017a)

Hsu, S.C., Jiao, Y., McAuliffe, M.J., Berisha, V., Wu, R.M., Levy, E.S.: Acoustic and perceptual speech characteristics of native Mandarin speakers with Parkinson's disease. J. Acoust. Soc. Am. **141**(3), EL293–EL299 (2017)

Whitfield, J.A., Mehta, D.D.: Examination of clear speech in Parkinson disease using measures of working vowel space. J. Speech Lang. Hear. Res. **62**(7), 2082–2098 (2019)

Kuo, C., Tjaden, K.: Acoustic variation during passage reading for speakers with dysarthria and healthy controls. J. Commun. Disord. **62**, 30–44 (2016)

Bang, Y.I., Min, K., Sohn, Y.H., Cho, S.R.: Acoustic characteristics of vowel sounds in patients with Parkinson disease. NeuroRehabilitation **32**(3), 649–654 (2013)

Kang, Y., Yoon, K.C., Lee, H.S., Seong, C.J.: A comparison of parameters of acoustic vowel space in patients with Parkinson's disease. Phonetics Speech Sci. **2**(4), 185–192 (2010)

Rusz, J., et al.: Imprecise vowel articulation as a potential early marker of Parkinson's disease effect of speaking task. J. Acoust. Soc. Am. **134**(3), 2171–2181 (2013)

Tjaden, K., Lam, J., Wilding, G.: Vowel acoustics in Parkinson's disease and multiple sclerosis: comparison of clear, loud, and slow speaking conditions. J. Speech Lang. Hear. Res. **56**(5), 1485–1502 (2013)

Watson, P.J., Munson, B.: Parkinson's disease and the effect of lexical factors on vowel articulation. J. Acoust. Soc. Am. **124**(5), EL291–EL295 (2008)

Sapir, S., Spielman, J.L., Ramig, L.O., Story, B.H., Fox, C.: Effects of intensive voice treatment (the Lee silverman voice treatment [LSVT]) on vowel articulation in dysarthric individuals with idiopathic Parkinson disease: acoustic and perceptual findings. J. Speech Lang. Hear. Res. **50**(4), 899–912 (2007)

Weismer, G., Jeng, J.Y., Laures, J.S., Kent, R.D., Kent, J.F.: Acoustic and intelligibility characteristics of sentence production in neurogenic speech disorders. Folia Phoniatr. Logopaedica **53**(1), 1–18 (2001)

Bunton, K., Keintz, C.K.: The use of a dual-task paradigm for assessing speech intelligibility in clients with Parkinson disease. J. Med. Speech-Lang. Pathol. **16**(3), 141–155 (2008)

Goberman, A.M., Elmer, L.W.: Acoustic analysis of clear versus conversational speech in individuals with Parkinson disease. J. Commun. Disord. **38**(3), 215–230 (2005)

Mefferd, A.: Tongue-and jaw-specific contributions to increased vowel acoustic contrast in response to slow, loud, and clear speech in talkers with dysarthria. J. Acoust. Soc. Am. **142**(4), 2640–2641 (2017)

Tjaden, K., Sussman, J.E., Wilding, G.E.: Impact of clear, loud, and slow speech on scaled intelligibility and speech severity in Parkinson's disease and multiple sclerosis. J. Speech Lang. Hear. Res. **57**(3), 779–792 (2014)

Picheny, M.A., Durlach, N.I., Braida, L.D.: Speaking clearly for the hard of hearing II: acoustic characteristics of clear and conversational speech. J. Speech Lang. Hear. Res. **29**(4), 434–446 (1986)

Lam, J., Tjaden, K., Wilding, G.: Acoustics of clear speech: effect of instruction. J. Speech Lang Hear. Res. **55**(6), 1807–1821 (2012)

Krause, J.C., Braida, L.D.: Investigating alternative forms of clear speech: the effects of speaking rate and speaking mode on intelligibility. J. Acoust. Soc. Am. **112**(5), 2165–2172 (2002)

Krause, J.C., Braida, L.D.: Acoustic properties of naturally produced clear speech at normal speaking rates. J. Acoust. Soc. Am. **115**(1), 362–378 (2004)

Adams, S.G., Weismer, G., Kent, R.D.: Speaking rate and speech movement velocity profiles. J. Speech Lang. Hear. Res. **36**(1), 41–54 (1993)

Dromey, C., Ramig, L.O., Johnson, A.B.: Phonatory and articulatory changes associated with increased vocal intensity in Parkinson disease: a case study. J. Speech Lang. Hear. Res. **38**(4), 751–764 (1995)

Gravelin, A.C., Whitfield, J.A.: Effect of clear speech on the duration of silent intervals at syntactic and phonemic boundaries in the speech of individuals with Parkinson disease. Am. J. Speech-Lang. Pathol. **28**(2S), 793–806 (2019)

Neel, A.T.: Effects of loud and amplified speech on sentence and word intelligibility in Parkinson disease. J. Speech Lang. Hear. Res. **52**(4), 1021–1033 (2009)

Tjaden, K., Martel-Sauvageau, V.: Consonant acoustics in Parkinson's disease and multiple sclerosis: comparison of clear and loud speaking conditions. Am. J. Speech-Lang. Pathol. **26** (2S), 569–582 (2017)

Tjaden, K., Wilding, G.E.: Effect of rate reduction and increased loudness on acoustic measures of anticipatory coarticulation in multiple sclerosis and Parkinson's disease. J. Speech Lang. Hear. Res. **48**(2), 261–277 (2005)

Whitfield, J.A., Dromey, C., Palmer, P.: Examining acoustic and kinematic measures of articulatory working space: effects of speech intensity. J. Speech Lang. Hear. Res. **61**(5), 1104–1117 (2018c)

Ho, A.K., Iansek, R., Bradshaw, J.L.: The effect of a concurrent task on Parkinsonian speech. J. Clin. Exp. Neuropsychol. **24**(1), 36–47 (2002)

O'Shea, S., Morris, M.E., Iansek, R.: Dual task interference during gait in people with Parkinson disease: effects of motor versus cognitive secondary tasks. Phys. Ther. **82**(9), 888–897 (2002)

Plummer-D'Amato, P., Altmann, L.J., Reilly, K.: Dual-task effects of spontaneous speech and executive function on gait in aging: exaggerated effects in slow walkers. Gait Post. **33**(2), 233–237 (2011)

Whitfield, J.A., Goberman, A.M.: Speech motor sequence learning: effect of Parkinson disease and normal aging on dual-task performance. J. Speech Lang. Hear. Res. **60**(6S), 1752–1765 (2017b)

Whitfield, J.A., Kriegel, Z., Fullenkamp, A.M., Mehta, D.D.: Effects of concurrent manual task performance on connected speech acoustics in individuals with Parkinson disease. J. Speech Lang. Hear. Res. **62**(7), 2099–2117 (2019)

Hornykiewicz, O.: Biochemical aspects of Parkinson's disease. Neurology **51**(2 Suppl 2), S2–S9 (1998)

Orozco-Arroyave, J. R., et al.: Towards an automatic monitoring of the neurological state of Parkinson's patients from speech. In: 2016 IEEE International Conference on Acoustics, Speech and Signal Processing (ICASSP), pp. 6490–6494. IEEE (March 2016)

A Review of the Use of Prosodic Aspects of Speech for the Automatic Detection and Assessment of Parkinson's Disease

Laureano Moro-Velazquez$^{(\boxtimes)}$ (iD) and Najim Dehak (iD)

Center for Language and Speech Processing, Johns Hopkins University,
Baltimore, MD 21218, USA
laureano@jhu.edu

Abstract. Several aspects of a person's speech can be influenced by Parkinson's Disease (PD), namely, phonatory, articulatory, prosodic, and cognitive-linguistic aspects. Several studies in literature extract information about these aspects to automatically detect or assess PD employing corpora containing different speech tasks from patients and control subjects. In this review, we analyze the influence of PD in the prosodic aspect and the potential use of prosody-related features in automatic detection and assessment of PD. Moreover, a list of corpora identified during the review, and an analysis of their characteristics are included in this article. As a conclusion of the review, we observe that the use of only prosody-related features in automatic detectors is uncommon in contrast to other aspects such as the phonatory and articulatory. Moreover, despite the clear evidence of the influence of PD in prosody, most of the proposed objective biomarkers or measures are not employed in the clinical practice to detect PD since a high percentage of the studies in literature only show trends and do not establish normative data for PD detection.

1 Introduction

Although there are several studies describing the speech of patients with Parkinson's Disease (PD) since 1950 [34,61], it is not until 1969 [16,17] that a group of researchers analyzed more completely the problems of phonation, prosody, and articulation of PD patients. Since then, the literature presents a large number of studies and approaches trying to identify the changes caused by PD in the voice or speech of patients, proposing the creation of new biomarkers or automatic detectors to support the diagnosis of this condition. To this respect, literature can be categorized and divided into four groups depending on the analyzed speech aspect: phonatory, articulatory, prosodic, and cognitive-linguistic. Each of these aspects could be subdivided, at the same time, into further dimensions. For instance, phonatory aspects can be related to the phonation activity (source) or the resonant cavities configuration. The prosodic aspect can be studied observing the speech rate, intonation, accentuation, and regularity while the

© Springer Nature Switzerland AG 2020
J. I. Godino-Llorente (Ed.): AAPS 2019, CCIS 1295, pp. 42–59, 2020.
https://doi.org/10.1007/978-3-030-65654-6_3

articulatory aspect's approaches focus on the segments' length, transitions analysis, or phonetics, among others. The cognitive-linguistic studies analyze the speaker's response to certain stimuli, the repetition of words, use of vocabulary, or use of formulaic expressions. It is common to find publications that combine or study several dimensions of one aspect while not too many analyze the combination of several aspects. In parallel, respiration is also affected by PD, and some studies address its effects in speech through its influence on the phonatory and prosodic aspects [59, 75].

Among the studies evaluating a patient's speech and voice, we can differentiate between perceptual and objective assessments, depending on the type of evaluation. In the perceptual assessment, qualified raters follow a particular protocol such as Frenchay dysarthria assessment [19], or Consensus Auditory Perceptual Evaluation of Voice (CAPE-V) [36] to perceptually assess the quality of the speech and voice of the speakers. On the other hand, the objective assessments use algorithms and signal processing techniques to characterize the speech signal. From the studies found in literature performing an objective assessment of the speech of people with PD, some propose measurements or features that can be used for diagnosis or that correlate with the severity of the disease. Others propose automatic detectors to distinguish between speakers with and without PD, or to predict the disease stage automatically. In this respect, the phonatory studies usually employ sustained vowels to measure features as noise, frequency, and amplitude perturbation, fundamental frequency, or formants frequency that under certain circumstances can also be measured on running speech. The studies framed within the prosodic and articulatory aspects are based on the feature extraction from connected speech, or the processing of specific segments of the speech. The cognitive-linguistic studies also employ running speech but are focused on semantic dimensions rather than on the acoustic signal.

In this article, we review different methodologies related to the analysis and characterization of the prosodic aspect in speakers for the detection and assessment of PD using speech. The main signal processing techniques that have been explored to provide new prosodic biomarkers and to assess the grade of affection of the disease are outlined. The motivation is to analyze the potential of prosody in automatic detection and assessment approaches since this aspect, along with the cognitive-linguistic aspect, has remained almost unexplored in this type of approach. Moreover, an analysis of some studies employing the prosodic aspect in combination with other aspects to detect or assess PD automatically is also included. Finally, a review of corpora containing speech from people with PD is included to illustrate common practices in these types of works.

The article is structured as follows. Section 2 includes a description of the studies related to prosodic aspects, while Sect. 3 describes studies combining the prosodic aspect with the phonatory or articulatory ones. Section 4 lists and describes different corpora including speech from speakers with PD and finally Sect. 5 includes a discussion.

2 Prosodic Aspects and Its Potential for the Automatic Detection and Assessment of Parkinson's Disease

2.1 Evidence of the Influence of PD in Prosody: Fundamental Frequency and Speech Sound Pressure Level

Attending to the studies found in literature about the prosody of speakers with PD, two main features, fundamental frequency, and speech Sound Pressure Level (SPL), and their related features are analyzed in a significant amount of studies since these are the two of the most characteristic acoustic traits associated to that aspect.

Although the early studies alluding to prosody on parkinsonian speech describe it as monotonous and with reduced loudness [45], one of the first articles performing objective measurements to characterize dysprosody or aprosody on patients [13] does not show relevant differences in speech SPL (mean values and variability) between the 17 patients and 17 studied controls. However, authors find evidence of higher fundamental frequency and a reduced pitch range in patients respect to controls. In a subsequent article [30], authors perform acoustic measurements of prosody in a read sentence and a short recording of spontaneous speech from 10 male patients and 10 male controls showing a higher fundamental frequency and a reduced speech SPL range in patients.

In an early study performing prosody measurements in untreated patients [32], the authors measure frequency and speech SPL variability over sentences from 22 PD patients and 28 controls, finding a dynamic range at a natural frequency similar for both, patients and controls. However, in a questionnaire administered to the same patients, these claim to suffer from monopitch, low SPL, and tremulousness. One of the reasons for the difference between the self-perception and the objective measurements is that for the prosodic analysis, this study only considers a read sentence and not spontaneous speech. The results on other early studies employing objective measurements [27] do not find significant differences between groups using declarative, affectively neutral sentences, being in concordance with the previously mentioned study [32].

In contrast, other more recent publications [66] find a reduced standard deviation of fundamental frequency and an elevated mean in male speakers and a significantly reduced standard deviation of fundamental frequency in female speakers, with no changes in mean values. In that study, four complex sentences are employed as speech tasks, including a main clause and a subordinate clause. Similar conclusions are obtained in subsequent studies [55] analyzing fundamental frequency standard deviation and mean values [31] in monologues.

In this sense, other study finds differences between patients and controls when asking speakers to perform diverse intonations of vowels (rising and falling intonation), reporting a more restricted range of fundamental frequency in patients (20 subjects) in comparison to controls (15 subjects) [35]. The same study also considers several linguistic modes for the used sentences as neutral, declarative, interrogative, and imperative to include distinct types of prosodic ranges. In fact, the differences between groups were only observable in declarative and interrogative modes. In the same sense, another study [37] finds a reduced fundamental frequency standard deviation for patients (10 subjects) respecting controls (20 subjects), especially in interrogative sentences. A reduced fundamental frequency and speech SPL variability has also been reported in patients in an advanced stage when analyzing monologues [53]. In this last study, the maximum phonation frequency range extracted from a singing scale task is the feature that best differentiates between patients (early and advanced stages) and controls. Regarding emotions, a reduced speech SPL range in patients has also been reported [44] when analyzing utterances produced in several emotional modes (neutral, happy, and sad).

It is important to note that these prosody indicators, like many others in the literature, have not been deeply studied during the prodromal period of many patients. To this respect, a study [25] makes use of the recordings of two individuals (one with PD and a matched control) appearing on an American television news services during 11 years. The analysis of the recordings, including 7 years of pre-diagnosis samples and 3 years of post-diagnosis, reveals that changes on fundamental frequency variability can be noticed 5 years before diagnosis. All the same, a study [26] on four speakers (two patients and two controls) along 10 years reports lower fundamental frequency variability in patients, even before clinical diagnosis. The same study suggests that Voice Onset Time (VOT) tends to be longer in patients in a middle stage.

Regarding the combination of speech SPL and fundamental frequency ranges, some authors suggest using phonetograms to compare patients and controls [70], which can be employed in automatic detection systems and, at the same time, can provide visual and easily explainable information to clinicians.

Other features related to fundamental frequency, as the Relative Fundamental Frequency (RFF), are found to be significantly reduced in patients (in ON and OFF states) with respect to controls [68], a feature which tends to be lower as the disease advances. This measurement reflects the variability of the instantaneous fundamental frequency around voiceless consonants (calculated using 10 cycles) respect to the reference fundamental frequency (calculated with a higher number of cycles, typically, 200). Therefore, a reduction of RFF implies a reduction of prosodic variability around articulation instants.

In the same manner, another sign found in some patients with PD is the difficulty to appropriately control the speech loudness in the presence of background noise [29], in contrast to speakers without PD, who can produce a higher speech SPL in accordance to the background noise (a mechanism known as Lombard effect [40].)

Consequently, a considerable number of studies find disprosodic characteristics in speakers with PD related to speech SPL (mainly, reduced overall level and reduced ranges and/or variability) [3,13,21,28–30,44,53,71,72] and to the fundamental frequency (mainly, reduced ranges and/or variability) [13,20,25,26,35,42,53,55,66,68]. However, some other publications [4,27,32] do not find any fundamental frequency variability difference between groups.

Nevertheless, this variability seems to be highly dependent on the speech task used. From the cited studies that do not find differences between patients and controls, one employs 12 declarative and affectively neutral utterances [27], other, a single neutral sentence [32] and the third only uses the repetition of a short neutral sentence [4]. Conversely, the studies finding significant differences in fundamental frequency variability between parkinsonian and control speakers include monologues or sentences in different linguistic modes (e.g., imperative or interrogative) or emotional modes (e.g., happy, sad or angry).

In this sense, although many studies find statistically significant differences between fundamental frequency and speech SPL-related features in patients and controls, that does not necessarily mean that these features can be used in diagnosis or detection of PD. These differences confirm trends in speakers with and without PD, but no studies are suggesting that the use of the cited prosodic features alone is clearly advisable to differentiate between groups with high accuracy. The reason is that in most of the studies, the prosodic feature distributions for the studied groups (patients and controls) are highly overlapped.

2.2 Speech Rate in Speakers with PD

One of the first comparisons of the speech rate between speakers with and without PD (17 subjects per group) [13] finds similar mean speech rate in both groups, being the standard deviation higher in the parkinsonian group. This higher variability is caused by some patients with a very low and others with a high speech rate compared to the control group, which is more homogeneous in this regard. Subtle differences in the speech rates between patients and controls have also been reported [41], suggesting a tendency to a lower mean rate in patients, while other studies suggest that the differences in speech rate of both groups are not significant [3,12,67]. In particular, authors of one of these latter studies [67], which analyzes the speech of 121 patients and 70 controls, consider that their conclusions differ from other previous studies since those use small corpora or different methodologies, which leads to inconsistent comparisons. The same authors report a higher acceleration at the end of long sentences in patients and a significant reduction of the total number of pauses, and point out a problem that is left unattended: no depression analysis is made in any of the patients for most of the studies, which could influence the results.

On the other hand, a more recent article [57] proposes a new algorithm to measure speech rate in dysarthric speakers. By using this algorithm, authors observe an increased pace acceleration in PD patients respect to controls.

In general, it can be said that there is a certain controversy in literature concerning speech rate, as different studies [2,3,12,13,20,41,42,67] report higher, lower, or the same rate in parkinsonian patients in comparison to control subjects. In this respect, as concluded in the review published by Blanchet et al. about the deficits in speech rate of speakers with PD [7], their speech rate is different to controls' speech in most of the cases. It can be faster, or slower, and, frequently, with higher variability. Additionally, the same authors point out that patients have more severe difficulties in modifying the speech rate when necessary. In a subsequent review [65], Skodda supports the same idea and suggests that the use of speech rate can be useful to monitor the evolution of the disease, as this feature shows a deterioration during the course of the disease.

2.3   Other Prosodic Indicators

Other studies found in the literature focus on characteristics directly linked with prosody such as breath control, the emphasis of syllables during speaking, pause duration, or even perception of prosody. To this respect, unorthodox breath pauses while speaking (agrammatical boundaries), as well as speech initiation at low lung volume, have been reported in some PD patients in comparison to controls [4, 11]. Also, longer pauses between sentences in a sentence repetition task and a lower percentage of speech time for each repetition have been found in a study with 20 patients and 19 controls [4].

Regarding the causes of the differences in prosody between patients and controls, a study [24] suggests an abnormal somatosensory laryngeal function in patients (19 subjects) in comparison to controls (18 subjects), associated with the timing of phonatory onset, respiratory driving pressure or lung volume employed per syllable. The study suggests that PD produces somatosensory laryngeal deficits that can lead to phonatory, articulatory and prosodic abnormalities, given that these somatosensory mechanisms -as well as the auditory- provide the feedback to produce the accurate adjustments necessary for a correct phonation, articulation, and prosody. In other words, there are some deficits in the basal ganglia's integration of the stimuli received in the sensory cells while speaking -or swallowing- deriving in a malfunction of voice and speech mechanisms. Subsequently, that study concludes that the abnormalities in the laryngeal somatosensory function produce deficits in the control of pitch and voice intensity and points out that these abnormalities may also increase the sensitivity of the auditory system during the speech, magnifying the self-perception of the vocal intensity and resulting in a decreased sound pressure level.

Respecting accentuation and phonemic stress[1], some studies [15, 50] suggest no differences in prosodic comprehension between patients and controls. However, in one of these studies [15] patients (30 subjects) demonstrated to have problems with the mechanisms involved in the pronunciation of noun compounds. In general, controls (15 subjects) made a clear distinction between noun phrases (e.g., green house) and noun compounds (e.g., Greenhouse) while patients failed to perform the prosodic actions to differentiate the two types of utterances (authors measure pitch and pauses between words, mainly).

A general reduction in emotion recognition and the ability of patients to identify the linguistic and affective meaning of sentences compared to controls has also been reported [38, 50, 51, 63].

---

[1] The phonemic stress can be defined as the relative emphasis given to one syllable respect to the others within a word, which can be caused by changes in the fundamental frequency and an increased loudness as well as a more precise articulation and increased vowel length. In some contexts, the term stress is substituted by accent.

3   Combined Approaches

Some of the most recent publications about automatic detection and assessment of PD from speech utilize the knowledge and biomarkers generated along the years about the four mentioned aspects (phonatory, articulatory, prosodic, and cognitive-linguistic) and combine them in their proposals. An overview of those considered as the most relevant and employing the prosodic aspect is included in this section.

Literature suggests that given that PD affects individual subsystems, these can affect several aspects simultaneously. For instance, the disturbances in phonatory and respiratory systems will impact prosody and articulation at the same time [54]. The study [54] is an example of the combination of prosodic, phonatory and articulatory aspects into an automatic classification system providing 90% accuracy distinguishing speakers with PD from controls. On that approach, 4 phonatory, 5 articulatory and 10 prosodic features are selected from a larger group by studying their statistical significance in PD detection and the correlation between features. Statistically insignificant features are removed, and only one group of measurements is selected. Each of these selected features is utilized in a separate classifier based on the Wald task [62], where the output scores are –1 if the measurements match the control group performance, 1 in the case of PD and 0 for indecisive situations. This methodology can be useful in a clinical environment since the measurements are easily interpretable, and it permits to have individual scores for each speech task, for each speech aspect and a global value. Additionally, the used corpus is highly relevant as it mainly contains speech from untreated patients in an early stage. The main drawback of the study is that there is no robust validation methodology as the same data is used to select the features and train the models and, therefore, the models can be over-fitted to the corpus so that results could be over-optimistic.

A very similar methodology is detailed in a subsequent study [55], where 6 phonetic, 4 articulatory and 3 prosodic features are measured in different speech tasks on 19 patients before and after starting pharmacological treatment and in 19 controls. In this case, results suggest that almost 90% of patients improve in at least one of the studied aspects of speech after treatment. Furthermore, an analysis of the correlation between these measures and Unified Parkinson's Disease Rating Scale (UPDRS) global scores reveals no statistically significant correlation.

A combination of prosodic, articulatory, and phonatory features has been proposed in [9] along with an automatic classification system for PD detection. In this approach, the authors use several speech tasks in German from 88 patients and 88 controls. Prosodic features are calculated from voiced segments and include statistics (mean, maximum, minimum, and standard deviation) from a group of typical acoustic measures including fundamental frequency, relative speech SPL, and segment duration. The articulatory features consist of Gaussian Mixture Model (GMM) mean vectors (one per utterance) obtained from Mel-Frequency Cepstral Coefficients (MFCC). Phonatory features include parameters of a physical glottis approximation of a two-mass vocal folds model described in [69]. Additionally, 1582 features from OpenSMILE are used too as a brute-force approach. All of these features are included in four separate classifiers using Support Vector Machine (SVM) with a linear kernel. Each type of feature is studied separately, and an unweighted score-level fusion is performed to evaluate the fusion of the four systems (three speech aspects). The best results (82% accuracy) are obtained using the articulatory approach (in a Leave One Out (LOO) validation scheme), while no improvements are reported by the fusion of systems. Authors also predict UPDRS scores divided into only three levels (low, medium, and high) by using the same features and speech tasks, obtaining no more than 60% accuracy.

Finally, most of the works performing severity prediction (UPDRS or Hoehn & Yahr (H-Y)), where [5, 22] are two examples, use a blend of features and/or tasks which can be considered a combined approach. For instance, [5] reports a mean absolute error of 5.5 on the UPDRS of 168 patients, employing MFCC, jitter, shimmer, and other features calculated with openSMILE as features, and suggests that the reading task is more appropriate for the prediction than sustained vowels or Diadochokinetik (DDK) tasks.

4 Analysis of Corpora Containing Speech from Patients with Parkinson's Disease

In this section, we list several parkinsonian speech corpora identified during the review, their content, advantages, and some methodological issues related to these. Table 1 includes a list of the most relevant corpora mentioned in this article, along with other corpora found containing speech tasks that allow prosody analysis. The table references the first study describing the correspondent corpus, the year of publication, the corpus' language, the number of patients and controls, the type of parkinsonism of the patients, and the speech tasks recorded. One of the reasons why this table is included here is to provide an extended view about the cited corpora in this article, making it easier to establish a comparative of the characteristics of each corpus and, hence, of the studies using them. The table allows to make a more reasoned comparison of the conclusions extracted for each study as different studies analyze a different number of speakers and employ different speech tasks. In some cases, subsequent studies refer to these same recordings and cite the original publication to describe the corpus but then use a different number of patients and/or speech tasks, not present in the original document. For instance, the study [66] describes for the first time a corpus containing 138 patients and 50 controls from which authors recorded four read sentences. However, the subsequent work [48] uses this corpus and refers to it as "the corpus described in [66]" but in this new study, 88 patients and 88 controls are part of the corpus while performing more speaking tasks as sustained vowels or monologues. This means that, although Table 1 makes a description of some corpora, in some cases authors expand their characteristics in subsequent studies.

It is important to note that, to the knowledge of the authors of the present article, almost no corpus of the listed is publicly available. Only [10,18,46,60] can be downloaded from a website. However, it is possible to find some authors willing to collaborate and to share the recordings that they retrieved under certain conditions or in exchange for certain compensation.

Methodological Issues: Recording Conditions. The recording of a voice and speech corpus to study a pathology must fulfill some requirements to avoid undesired effects such as an excessive influence of the channel in the audio, leading to biased studies or models. For example, some corpora identified in Table 1 have been recorded in sound-treated booths. The fact that a booth is acoustically insulated does not mean that the acoustic conditioning, and therefore, the acoustic field inside the booth, is the most adequate to record voice signals. Mainly, most of these cabins are designed to perform audiometry, especially when its plant does not exceed 8m^2, and it includes a glass panel to allow interaction with the person administering the audiometry. These cabins generate a sound filtering that can cancel certain frequencies and over-enhance others. In some other cases, omnidirectional microphones are employed, allowing signals and reflections from all directions to be recorded (instead of using cardioid microphones that can be oriented to the mouth of the speaker and help avoiding some background noises).

A significant drawback of the corpora used in some of the revised publications is that recordings are performed using portable and multiple equipment, introducing noise and variability, which could interfere in the optimal training of models. The inclusion of noise and reverberation does not necessarily bias the results and can be included to study how these undesired conditions affect the performance of a system. However, the use of different acoustic environments for different classes (one acoustic environment for patients and a different one for controls) can lead to trained models in machine learning approaches that could be more focused in the acoustic environment than in the differences between the speech of these classes.

In the same way, the inclusion of speakers with organic pathologies could bias the results. For instance, control speakers with an organic pathology could be falsely accepted as a PD patient in an automatic detector due to their lower speech to noise ratio. To avoid this problem, some of the analyzed studies include a previous analysis of the speaker's larynx performed by a specialist or a hearing test to discard any organic pathology or hearing impairments that could influence the phonation or the speech. However, most of the studies only incorporate a survey to discard smokers or subjects with known vocal issues. Other articles perform a study of depression, which is commonly associated with PD and, in the same way, affects prosody. Without such a study, some of the prosodic biomarkers found in patients could be more related to depression than to mechanisms directly associated with PD.

After examining the literature, it is also possible to observe that many of the studies use speech corpora from patients under pharmacological treatment. As these therapies could influence results, some of the studies analyze the influence

Table 1. Parkinsonian speech corpora identified in literature.

Year	Study	Lang.	# Speakers	Pathologies	Type of material
1978	[39]	American English	200 patients	Idiopathic PD and postencephalitic PD	Read sentences and from 3 to 5 min of conversational speech
1988	[30]	American English	10 patients, 10 controls	PD-not specified	Read passage and spontaneous speech
1988	[15]	American English	30 patients, 15controls	Idiopathic PD	16 noun compounds and 16 paired noun phrases. Image description
1993	[27]	German	12 patients, 12 controls	Idiopathic PD (7), Huntingtons Disease (5)	12 declarative and affectively neutral utterances
1997	[21]	American English	30 patients, 14 controls	Idiopathic PD	Sustained vowels, monologue and picture description
1997	[32]	Spanish	22 patients, 28 controls	not specified	A sustained vowel and a read sentence
1998	[37]	French	20 patients, 20 controls	Idiopathic PD (10), Friedreich's Ataxia (10)	40 read sentences
1999	[28]	Australian English	200 patients	Idiopathic PD	2 min conversational speech
2000	[53]	Australian English	60 patients, 30 controls	Idiopathic PD	A sustained vowel, a singing up and down scale, 1 min monologue
2005	[11]	American English	7 patients, 6 controls	Idiopathic PD	Monologue. The recordings include additional data: measurements of kinematic information of the chest wall to determine respiratory movements
2008	[67]	German	121 patients, 70 controls	Idiopathic PD	4 complex sentences
2008	[44]	German	16 patients, 16 controls		Repetition of a word in different emotional intonations
2009	[23]	American English	52 patients	PD-not specified	Sustained vowels and two picture descriptions: with and without distractions. Although in the cited work, authors only refers to these patients and tasks, posterior studies citing this corpus (such as [5]) include much more patients and tasks
2011	[66]	German	138 patients, 50 controls	Idiopathic PD	4 sentences
2011	[74]	American English	16 patients and 16 controls	Idiopathic PD	6 sentences varying in length and syntactic complexity
2011	[14]	American English	10 patients (with DBS) and 12 controls	Idiopathic PD	DDK
2012	[1]	American English	32 patients and 32 controls	not specified	Rainbow passage and three repetitions of a read sentence. Patients are recorded in two sessions. One at least 9 h after medication intake (OFF) and other 45 min after medication intake (ON)
2013	[64]	German	80 patients, 60 controls	Idiopathic PD	1 sustained vowel and 4 sentences
2013	[52]	American English	15 patients, 15 controls	PD-not specified (8), Multi-system atrophy (1), Corticobasal degeneration (1), Friedrich's ataxia (3), Cerebellar toxicity (1) and unknown (1)	Syllable sequences, ranging from low to high complexity

(continued)

Table 1. (*continued*)

Year	Study	Lang.	# Speakers	Pathologies	Type of material
2013	[56]	Czech	20 patients, 15 controls (only male)	Idiopathic PD	Sustained vowels (/a/, /i/,/u/), sentence repetition, read passage and monologue
2013	[55]	Czech	19 patients, 19 controls	Idiopathic PD	1 sustained vowel, 4 sentences, 1 DDK task (/pa-ta-ka/) and 1 monologue
2013	[60]	Turkish	20 patients, 20 controls	not specified	26 samples, including sustained vowels, words, and short sentences
2013	[71]	American English	24 patients, 15 controls	13 Idiopathic PD, 11 multiple sclerosis	25 read sentences in habitual, clear, loud and slow conditions
2014	[49]	Colombian Spanish	50 patients, 50 controls	Idiopathic PD	Sustained vowels, DDK tests, isolated words, read sentences, read passages and 1 monologue
2015	[4]	Italian	20 patients, 19 controls	Idiopathic PD	10 repetitions of a specific read sentence
2016	[10]	-	1087 patients, 5581 controls	PD	Sustained vowel /a:/ and other speech unrelated registers such as tapping or walking
2017	[73]	Czech	48 patients, 16 controls	Idiopathic PD, progressive supranuclear palsy and multiple system atrophy	Several series of syllable sequences
2017	[18]	Italian	28 patients, 37 controls	Idiopathic PD	DDK tasks, sustained vowels, series of words and read texts
2018	[58]	Czech	80 patients, 30 controls	Idiopathic rapid eye movement sleep behavior disorder (50), Idiopathic PD (30)	Sustained vowel (/a/), DDK task (pa-ta-ka) and 90 s monologue about a short fictional story
2019	[46, 47]	Castillian Spanish	47 patients, 32 controls	Idiopathic PD	DDK tasks, sustained vowels, read texts and monologue (picture description)

of the treatment in a patient's speech. To this respect, authors of study [55] objectively analyze prosodic, phonatory, and articulatory features of 19 patients before starting a symptomatic treatment and between one and two years after the beginning of the dopaminergic therapy. A statistical analysis of these features reveals no significant differences between the two recording sessions. However, a second analysis employing pattern recognition techniques shows that some patients tend to be classified as controls after starting the pharmacological therapy, especially when utilizing some prosodic features related to speech SPL, and fundamental frequency variability as other articulatory and phonatory features.

Subjects and Materials. The number of speakers included in the studied corpora ranges from 2 to 1087. It is not possible to extract a clear conclusion on the minimum recommended number of subjects that a corpus should include since it all depends on the goals of the study using the recordings and the speech tasks to be used. What is clear is that the articles using a small number of subjects serve as case studies, but their conclusions cannot be considered as generalist or normative until other studies using more subjects can confirm them. In contrast, some collections of recordings such as the one used in [54], while containing a relatively small number of speakers (46, from which 23 are patients), are highly relevant as these include only newly diagnosed patients. In that corpus, none of the patients is under treatment, and the average time since diagnosis is 30 months.

The most significant differences among the articles analyzing the same aspect are, usually, the number of subjects, the stage of the disease and the type of speech tasks. These differences are the primary source of discrepancies between studies [67]. For instance, those containing interrogative sentences or in any emotional mode usually find more influence of PD in prosody than studies employing neutral sentences [35, 44].

In the same sense, a complete analysis of speakers' prosody would require several hours of recordings, including different emotional modes and contexts. As this is a complicated and costly task, some of the studies analyzing prosody ask speakers to read stories or texts containing different emotional modes to enrich the prosodic content. In general, these recordings do not include more than 30 min per patient. This indicates that most of the speech recordings of PD patients contain non-spontaneous emotional modes, and biomarkers obtained from spontaneous speech could be different. To this extent, only some articles analyze long-term recordings obtained from television broadcasting programs in which one of the speakers has PD [25].

Most of the studies focused on the detection of PD and using speech processing and machine learning technologies present speaker groups (usually, PD patients and controls) matched in number, age, and sex. This matching is crucial since age and sex influence the acoustic information of voice and speech by itself and, significant demographic differences between patients and controls in a corpus could bias the results.

Additionally, the influence of simultaneous tasks [76] has to be taken into account in studies observing the direct influence of PD in speech. For instance, as PD also affects vision [6], the prosody can be influenced by visual problems while reading. For this reason, some authors ask speakers to listen and repeat pre-recorded sentences instead of asking them to read texts [47], to discard the influence of PD in the eye movement while reading.

5 Discussion

In this review, we have analyzed the influence of PD in prosody as well as the use of prosodic-related features combined with other feature groups, in automatic PD detection or assessment schemes. Additionally, we have listed and analyzed different corpora that have been employed in representative studies referenced in this review, as well as some methodological issues associated with them.

One of the main findings related to prosody in speakers with PD is that there is a reduction of speech SPL or a reduction of SPL variability, as reported in multiple studies [3, 13, 21, 28–30, 44, 53, 71, 72]. Similarly, another feature family appearing in literature with remarkable results is the one related to fundamental frequency variability while speaking, where multiple studies report a reduced range in patients respect to controls [13, 20, 25, 26, 35, 42, 53, 55, 66, 68].

Regarding this frequency variability, measured from speech or phonatory tasks, there are almost no studies using singing tasks (one of the scarce examples found in literature is [53]). This type of task could be useful since it requires fundamental frequency changes, although intonation capabilities could be different in distinct individuals independently of their neurological state.

Concerning the used materials, speech tasks containing different linguistic modes such as interrogative or imperative, or emotional modes such as angry or happy, usually provide the best differentiation between patients and controls in most of the analyzed studies, especially in those related to fundamental frequency and speech SPL. In the same sense, the use of noun compounds and noun phrases (Greenhouse vs. green house) can provide extra information in the analysis of prosody of speakers with PD.

Additionally, the literature suggests that the variability on speech rate in groups of patients is usually higher than in controls. However, there is a certain controversy about the use of this type of feature since patients have a higher or lower speech rate than controls (and hence, there is higher variability), but there is no clear pattern to this respect.

Although articles are studying the voice and speech of patients since more than 50 years ago, it is not possible to find so far many clinical validation studies from the neurological service of any hospital using objective speech biomarkers or automatic classifiers employing speech as to support the diagnosis of idiopathic PD (to the authors of this article knowledge).

On the other hand, in this review we have analyzed combined approaches, that bring together features from two or more different aspects into a single scheme, merging the discriminative properties of each aspect. The main hypothesis of these approaches is that these properties can be somehow complementary and the combination can provide a synergistic scheme. Literature suggests that these types of approaches are the most appropriate to help clinicians on the differential diagnosis using speech as these can cover different types of motor (and non-motor, if linguistic aspects are considered) signs at the same time. To this respect, some of the latest systems proposed in the literature that combine several aspects allow to observe the results and features separately to permit clinicians to assess the influence of the disease on speech more precisely and to make more resonated decisions.

Although some early studies [39, 41, 77] point out that PD has a more explicit reflection on the phonation of patients than in articulation or prosody, more recent works [54] suggest that on early stages, prosody is the most affected speech aspect. Articles like [25] support the idea that prosody is affected since the prodromal period, although authors did not study other aspects but prosody. At the same time, other publications [8, 43] point out to cognitive impairments before the appearance of dysarthrophonic signs. Equally, studies analyzing articulatory aspects in newly diagnosed patients, provide excellent results in differentiating them from controls [48]. In general, although the influence of the disease in most of these aspects is noticeable in mid to advanced stages, there is no consensus on which aspect is more appropriate to help on differential diagnosis in early stages. Therefore, a potential solution is to use a combined approach, containing at least two aspects.

In the same sense, some articles indicate that text-dependent utterances and spontaneous speech can help better to obtain an accurate differentiation between patients and controls than other materials such as DDK tasks or sustained vowels [33]. However, the use of a speech task depends on the analyzed aspect and the feature to be measured. Sustained vowels and DDK tasks can be performed almost identically by patients with different mother tongues and can be utilized in language-independent methodologies.

Finally, despite all of this evidence, a small number of studies employ exclusively prosodic features to detect or assess PD automatically. This can be motivated by the fact that a reliable characterization of the prosodic aspect remains a challenging task to be explored. In the same sense, although many articles evidence the differences in some prosody features between speakers with and without PD, these differences only indicate trends. Most commonly, the distribution of these feature values is highly overlapped between patients and controls. To date, this does not allow us using only prosodic biomarkers to differentiate between these two groups with diagnosis purposes.

References

1. Stepp, C.E.: Relative fundamental frequency during vocal onset and offset in older speakers with and without Parkinson's disease. J. Acoustic Soc. Am. **133**(3), 1637–1643 (2012)
2. Ackermann, H., Konczak, J., Hertrich, I.: The temporal control of repetitive articulatory movements in parkinson's disease. Brain Lang. **56**(2), 312–319 (1997)
3. Walsh, B., Smith, A.: Basic parameters of articulatory movements and acoustics in individuals with parkinson's disease. Mov. Disord. **27**(7), 843–850 (2012)
4. Bandini, A., et al.: Automatic identification of dysprosody in idiopathic parkinson's disease. Biomed. Signal Process. Control **17**, 47–54 (2015)
5. Bayestehtashk, A., Asgari, M., Shafran, I., McNames, J.: Fully automated assessment of the severity of Parkinsonś disease from speech. Comput. Speech Lang. **29**(1), 172–185 (2015)
6. Biousse, V., Skibell, B., Watts, R., Loupe, D., Drews-Botsch, C., Newman, N.: Ophthalmologic features of parkinson's disease. Neurology **62**(2), 177–180 (2004)
7. Blanchet, P., Snyder, G.: Speech rate deficits in individuals with parkinson's disease: a review of the literature. J. Med. Speech Lang. Pathol. **17**(1), 1–7 (2009)
8. Bocanegra, Y., García, A.M., Pineda, D., Buriticá, O., Villegas, A., Lopera, F., Gómez, D., Gómez-Arias, C., Cardona, J.F., Trujillo, N., et al.: Syntax, action verbs, action semantics, and object semantics in parkinson's disease: Dissociability, progression, and executive influences. Cortex **69**, 237–254 (2015)
9. Bocklet, T., Steidl, S., Nöth, E., Skodda, S.: Automatic evaluation of parkinson's speech-acoustic, prosodic and voice related cues. In: Proceedings of the Annual Conference of the International Speech Communication Association, INTER-SPEECH (2013)
10. Bot, B.M., et al.: The mpower study, parkinson disease mobile data collected using researchkit. Scientific data **3**, 160011 (2016)

11. Bunton, K.: Patterns of lung volume use during an extemporaneous speech task in persons with Parkinson disease. J. Commun. Disord. **38**(5), 331–348 (2005)

12. Caligiuri, M.P.: The influence of speaking rate on articulatory hypokinesia in parkinsonian dysarthria. Brain Lang. **36**(3), 493–502 (1989)

13. Canter, G.J.: Speech characteristics of patients with Parkinson's disease: I intensity, pitch and duration. J. Speech Hear. Disord. **28**(3), 221–229 (1963)

14. Chenausky, K., MacAuslan, J., Goldhor, R.: Acoustic analysis of PD speech. Parkinson's Disease (2011)

15. Darkins, A.W., Fromkin, V.A., Benson, D.F.: A characterization of the prosodic loss in Parkinson's disease. Brain Lang. **34**(2), 315–327 (1988)

16. Darley, F.L., Aronson, A.E., Brown, J.R.: Clusters of deviant speech dimensions in the dysarthrias. J. Speech Hear. Res. **12**(3), 462–496 (1969)

17. Darley, F.L., Aronson, A.E., Brown, J.R.: Differential diagnostic patterns of dysarthria. J. Speech Lang. Hear. Res. **12**(2), 246 (1969)

18. Dimauro, G., Di Nicola, V., Bevilacqua, V., Caivano, D., Girardi, F.: Assessment of speech intelligibility in parkinson's disease using a speech-to-text system. IEEE Access **5**, 22199–22208 (2017)

19. Enderby, P.: Frenchay dysarthria assessment. British J. Disord. Commun. **15**(3), 165–173 (1980)

20. Flint, A.J., Black, S.E., Campbell-Taylor, I., Gailey, G.F., Levinton, C.: Acoustic analysis in the differentiation of parkinsoń disease and major depression. J. Psycholinguist. Res. **21**(5), 383–399 (1992)

21. Fox, C.M., Ramig, L.O.: Vocal sound pressure level and self-perception of speech and voice in men and women with idiopathic parkinson disease. Am. J. Speech-Lang. Pathol. **6**(2), 85–94 (1997)

22. Galaz, Z., Mzourek, Z., Mekyska, J., Smekal, Z.: Degree of parkinson's disease severity estimation based on speech signal processing. In: IEEE 39th International pp. 503–506 (2016)

23. Goetz, C.G., et al.: Testing objective measures of motor impairment in early parkinson's disease: feasibility study of an at-home testing device. Mov. Disord. **24**(4), 551–556 (2009)

24. Hammer, M.J., Barlow, S.M.: Laryngeal somatosensory deficits in parkinson's disease: implications for speech respiratory and phonatory control. Exp. Brain Res. **201**(3), 401–409 (2010)

25. Harel, B.T., Cannizzaro, M., Snyder, P.J.: Variability in fundamental frequency during speech in prodromal and incipient Parkinson's Disease: A longitudinal case study. Brain Cogn. **56**(1), 24–29 (2004)

26. Harel, B.T., Cannizzaro, M.S., Cohen, H., Reilly, N., Snyder, P.J.: Acoustic characteristics of Parkinsonian speech: A potential biomarker of early disease progression and treatment. J. Neurol. **17**(6), 439–453 (2004)

27. Hertrich, I., Ackermann, H.: Acoustic analysis of speech prosody in huntington's and parkinson's disease: a preliminary report. Clinical Ling. & Phone **7**(4), 285–297 (1993)

28. Ho, A.K., Iansek, R., Marigliani, C., Bradshaw, J.L., Gates, S.: Speech impairment in a large sample of patients with parkinson's disease. Behav. Neurol. **11**(3), 131–137 (1999)

29. Ho, A., Bradshaw, J., Iansek, R., Alfredson, R.: Speech volume regulation in Parkinson's disease: Effects of implicit cues and explicit instructions. Neuropsychologia (1999)

30. Illes, J., Metter, E., Hanson, W., Iritani, S.: Language production in Parkinson's Disease: Acoustic and linguistic considerations. Brain Lang. **33**(1), 146–160 (1988)

31. Illner, V., Sovka, P., Rusz, J.: Validation of freely-available pitch detection algorithms across various noise levels in assessing speech captured by smartphone in parkinson's disease. Biomed. Signal Process. Control **58**, 101831 (2020)
32. Jiménez-Jiménez, F.J., et al.: Acoustic voice analysis in untreated patients with parkinson's disease. Parkinsonism Related Disord. **3**(2), 111–116 (1997)
33. Jiménez-Monsalve, J.C., Vásquez-Correa, J.C., Orozco-Arroyave, J.R., Gomez-Vilda, P.: Phonation and articulation analyses in laryngeal pathologies, cleft lip and palate, and parkinson's disease. In: Ferrández Vicente, J.M., Álvarez-Sánchez, J.R., de la Paz López, F., Toledo Moreo, J., Adeli, H. (eds.) IWINAC 2017. LNCS, vol. 10338, pp. 424–434. Springer, Cham (2017). https://doi.org/10.1007/978-3-319-59773-7_43
34. Kaplan, H.A., Machover, S., Rabiner, A.: A study of the effectiveness of drug therapy in parkinsonism. J. Nerv. Ment. Dis. **119**(5), 398–411 (1954)
35. Kegl, J., Cohen, H., Poizner, H.: Articulatory consequences of Parkinson's disease: perspectives from two modalities. Brain Cogn. **40**(2), 355–86 (1999)
36. Kempster, G.B., Gerratt, B.R., Abbott, K.V., Barkmeier-Kraemer, J., Hillman, R.E.: Consensus auditory-perceptual evaluation of voice: development of a standardized clinical protocol. Am. J. Speech-Lang. Pathol. **18**(2), 124–132 (2009)
37. Le Dorze, G., Ryalls, J., Brassard, C., Boulanger, N., Ratte, D.: A comparison of the prosodic characteristics of the speech of people with parkinson's disease and friedreich's ataxia with neurologically normal speakers. Folia Phoniatrica et Logopaedica **50**(1), 1–9 (1998)
38. Lloyd, A.J.: Comprehension of prosody in parkinson's disease. Cortex **35**(3), 389–402 (1999)
39. Logemann, J.A., Fisher, H.B., Boshes, B., Blonsky, E.R.: Frequency and cooccurrence of vocal tract dysfunctions in the speech of a large sample of parkinson patients. J. Speech Hear. Disord. **43**(1), 47–57 (1978)
40. Lombard, E.: Le signe de l'elevation de la voix. Ann Maladies de L'Oreille et du Larynx **37**, 2 (1911)
41. Ludlow, C.L., Connor, N.P., Bassich, C.J.: Speech timing in parkinson's and huntington's disease. Brain Lang. **32**(2), 195–214 (1987)
42. Metter, E.J., Hanson, W.R.: Clinical and acoustical variability in hypokinetic dysarthria. J. Commun. Disord. **19**(5), 347–366 (1986)
43. Miller, N., Noble, E., Jones, D., Allcock, L., Burn, D.J.: How do i sound to me? perceived changes in communication in parkinson's disease. Clinical Rehabil. **22**(1), 14–22 (2008)
44. Mobes, J., Joppich, G., Stiebritz, F., Dengler, R., Schroder, C.: Emotional speech in Parkinson's disease. Mov. Disord. **23**(6), 824–829 (2008)
45. Monrad-Krohn, G.: The third element of speech: Prosody and its disorders. Problems in dynamic neurology pp. 101–118 (1963)
46. Moro-Velazquez, L., et al.: Phonetic relevance and phonemic grouping of speech in the automatic detection of parkinson's disease. Scientific Reports **9**(1), 1–16 (2019)
47. Moro-Velazquez, L., et al.: A forced gaussians based methodology for the differential evaluation of parkinson's disease by means of speech processing. Biomed. Signal Process. Control **48**, 205–220 (2019)
48. Orozco-Arroyave, J.R., et al.: Automatic detection of Parkinson's disease in running speech spoken in three different languages. J. Acous. Soc. Am. **139**(1), 481 (2016)
49. Orozco-Arroyave, J., Arias-Londoño, J.: New Spanish speech corpus database for the analysis of people suffering from Parkinson's disease (2014)

50. Pell, M.D.: On the receptive prosodic loss in parkinson's disease. Cortex **32**(4), 693–704 (1996)
51. Pell, M.D., Leonard, C.L.: Processing emotional tone from speech in Parkinson's disease: a role for the basal ganglia. Cogn. Affect Behav. Neurosci. **3**(4), 275–288 (2003)
52. Reilly, K.J., Spencer, K.A.: Sequence complexity effects on speech production in healthy speakers and speakers with hypokinetic or ataxic dysarthria. PloS one **8**(10), (2013)
53. Rhonda, J.H., Oates, J.M., Debbie, J.P., Andrew, J.H.: Voice characteristics in the progression of Parkinson's disease. Int. J. Lang. Commun. Disord. **35**(3), 407–418 (2000)
54. Rusz, J., Cmejla, R., Ruzickova, H., Ruzicka, E.: Quantitative acoustic measurements for characterization of speech and voice disorders in early untreated Parkinson's Disease. J. Acoust. Soc. Am. **129**(1), 350–367 (2011)
55. Rusz, J., et al.: Evaluation of speech impairment in early stages of parkinson's disease: a prospective study with the role of pharmacotherapy. J. Neural Trans. **120**(2), 319–329 (2013)
56. Rusz, J., et al.: Imprecise vowel articulation as a potential early marker of parkinson's disease: Effect of speaking task. J. Acoust. Soc. Am. **134**(3), 2171–2181 (2013)
57. Rusz, J., Hlavnicka, J., Cmejla, R., Ruzicka, E.: Automatic evaluation of speech rhythm instability and acceleration in dysarthrias associated with basal ganglia dysfunction. Front. BioEng. Biotechnol. **3** (2015)
58. Rusz, J., et al.: Smartphone allows capture of speech abnormalities associated with high risk of developing parkinson's disease. IEEE Trans. Neural Syst. Rehab. Eng. **26**(8), 1495–1507 (2018)
59. Sadagopan, N., Huber, J.E.: Effects of loudness cues on respiration in individuals with parkinson's disease. Mov. Disord. **22**(5), 651–659 (2007)
60. Sakar, B.E., et al.: Collection and analysis of a parkinson speech dataset with multiple types of sound recordings. IEEE J. Biomed. Health Inf. **17**(4), 828–834 (2013)
61. Sarno, M.: Speech impairment in parkinson's disease. Arch. Phys. Med. Rehabil. **49**(5), 269–275 (1968)
62. Schlesinger, M.I., Hlaváč, V.: Ten lectures on statistical and structural pattern recognition, vol. 24. Springer Science & Business Media (2013)
63. Schroder, C., et al.: Perception of emotional speech in parkinson's disease. Mov. Disord. **21**(10), 1774–1778 (2006)
64. Skodda, S., Grönheit, W., Mancinelli, N., Schlegel, U.: Progression of voice and speech impairment in the course of parkinson's disease: A longitudinal study. Parkinson's Disease **2013** (2013)
65. Skodda, S.: Aspects of speech rate and regularity in Parkinsonś disease. J. Neurol. Sci. **310**(1–2), 231–236 (2011)
66. Skodda, S., Grö, W., Schlegel, U., Grönheit, W., Schlegel, U.: Intonation and speech rate in parkinson's disease: general and dynamic aspects and responsiveness to levodopa admission. J. Voice **25**(4), e199–205 (2011)
67. Skodda, S., Schlegel, U.: Speech rate and rhythm in parkinson's disease. Mov. Disord. **23**(7), 985–992 (2008)
68. Stepp, C.E.: Relative fundamental frequency during vocal onset and offset in older speakers with and without Parkinson's disease. J. Acoust. Soc. Am. **133**(3), 1637–1643 (2013)
69. Stevens, K.N.: Acoustic phonetics, vol. 30. MIT press (2000)

70. Teston, B.: L'evaluation objective des dysfonctionnements de la voix et de la parole; 2e partie: les dysphonies. Travaux Interdisciplinaires du Laboratoire Parole et Langage d'Aix-en-Provence (TIPA) **20**, 169–232 (2001)

71. Tjaden, K., Lam, J., Wilding, G.: Vowel acoustics in Parkinson's Disease and multiple sclerosis: comparison of clear, loud, and slow speaking conditions. J. Speech Lang. Hear. Res. **56**(5), 1485–502 (2013)

72. Tjaden, K., Martel-Sauvageau, V.: Consonant acoustics in parkinson's disease and multiple sclerosis: comparison of clear and loud speaking conditions. Am. J. Speech-Lang. Pathol. **26**(2S), 569 (2017)

73. Tykalova, T., Rusz, J., Klempir, J., Cmejla, R., Ruzicka, E.: Distinct patterns of imprecise consonant articulation among Parkinson's disease, progressive supranuclear palsy and multiple system atrophy. Brain Lang. **165**, 1–9 (2017)

74. Walsh, B., Smith, A.: Linguistic complexity, speech production, and comprehension in parkinsons disease: Behavioral and physiological indices. J. Speech, Lang. Hear. Res. **54**(3), 787–802 (2011)

75. Wang, C.M., Shieh, W.Y., Weng, Y.H., Hsu, Y.H., Wu, Y.R.: Non-invasive assessment determine the swallowing and respiration dysfunction in early parkinson's disease. Parkinsonism & Related Disord. **42**, 22–27 (2017)

76. Whitfield, J.A., Goberman, A.M.: Speech motor sequence learning: Effect of parkinson disease and normal aging on dual-task performance. J. Speech Lang. Hear. Res. **60**(6S), 1752–1765 (2017)

77. Zwirner, P., Barnes, G.J.: Vocal tract steadiness: a measure of phonatory and upper airway motor control during phonation in dysarthria. J. Speech Lang. Hear. Res. **35**(4), 761–768 (1992)

Automatic Processing of Aerodynamic Parameters in Parkinsonian Dysarthria

Clara Ponchard[1]([✉]) [iD], Alain Ghio[2] [iD], Lise Crevier Buchman[1] [iD],
and Didier Demolin[1] [iD]

[1] Laboratoire de Phonétique et Phonologie,
UMR 7018, Sorbonne Nouvelle, Paris 3, France
cponchard@yahoo.fr
[2] Aix-Marseille Université, CNRS, LPL, UMR 7309, Aix-En-Provence, France

Abstract. Currently, perceptual evaluation remains the standard used in clinical practice for the diagnosis and therapeutic monitoring of Parkinson's patients. However, this approach is recognized as subjective, non-reproducible and time-consuming. These limitations make it unsuitable for large corpora or for the follow-up of the progression of the condition of dysarthric patients. Faced with these limitations, professionals express their need for objective methods to assessing dysarthric speech. However, predicting the UPDRS score from speech signals is a complex task that still achieves poor results. The aim of this study is to analyze variations of intra- oral pressure at different measurement points according to several controlled constraints (sex, age, duration of the disease, pharmacological status of the patients, degree of severity of the dysarthria) in order to assess if it is a relevant indicator of Parkinsonian dysarthria that could be taken into account to improve the prediction of the UPDRS score from speech signals. We also present a segmentation method applicable to pathological speech based on the measurement of RMS intensity and intra-oral pressure. This method could improve the constraints that are inherent in human annotation tasks for pathological speech such as subjectivity and non- reproducibility. This criterion will make it possible to homogenize the segmentation of human experts but it can also be exploited by automatic alignment systems.

Keywords: Aerodynamics · Dysarthria · Automatic speech processing · Automatic speech alignment

1 Introduction

Speakers with Parkinson's disease suffer from hypokinetic dysarthria which manifests itself in all aspects of speech production; breathing, phonation, articulation, nasalization and prosody. In view of the extent of the dysfunctions, we have focused our work on the articulatory aspect of speech and more precisely on the disturbance characteristics of stop consonants. Indeed, articulatory studies [1–3] on the production of Parkinsonian speech show that the realization of bilabial stop consonants is particularly impaired in Parkinsonian subjects. Their realization is described as imprecise [4] even indistinct [5]. These stop consonants are often realized as fricatives and constitute a

© Springer Nature Switzerland AG 2020
J. I. Godino-Llorente (Ed.): AAPS 2019, CCIS 1295, pp. 60–76, 2020.
https://doi.org/10.1007/978-3-030-65654-6_4

typical articulatory modification of Parkinson's disease [6]. These articulatory modifications disturb the processing of data collected from Parkinsonian subjects, in particular the segmentation and extraction of acoustic measurements. One of the aims of this work is to provide a conceptual and methodological framework for segmenting these data and applying automatic processes to find reliable acoustic and aerodynamic cues. Indeed, it is essential to link the aerodynamic phase and the acoustic phase because the acoustic phase helps to estimate the product of the aerodynamic phase and, more importantly, is one of the main sources of information or inferences about the subsequent receptive and perceptual phases. The aerodynamic phase of speech is important since it is at this stage that speech sounds are generated. It's the link between the speaker's bodily activity allowing shape changes in the articulatory phase and the resulting sound waves (in the acoustic phase).

According to Baken and Orlikoff [7] speech sounds are the product of accurate use of the air pressure generated by the respiratory system. It is often useful to know the air pressure in a given region of the vocal tract (particularly in relation to the pressure at another location) and, more importantly, to observe the changes in air pressure values that result from vocal activity. These observations, combined with an understanding of the structure and function of the vocal tract, allow clinician to infer much about the nature and degree of speech abnormality. However, aerodynamic parameters are very rarely used in studies to evaluate voice in Parkinson's disease, unlike acoustic measurements, which are an obvious choice for patient evaluation. The aim of this study is therefore to define a model of the intraoral pressure of Parkinson's production in relation to healthy subjects. To do this, we use aerodynamic parameters to distinguish patients from controls and examine the effects of L-DOPA treatment on voice.

2 Methodology

2.1 Patients and Subjects

The data examined in this study is a subset of the AHN corpus which includes sound and aerodynamic recordings of 990 patients and 160 age-matched controls [8]. This corpus is largely composed of patients recordings with Parkinson's disease (601) and Parkinson's syndromes (98) that have been examined in a number of studies [9–14].

The subset chosen for this study consists of recordings collected from six Parkinson's patients, three women and three men, all native French speakers. These patients were treated with L-DOPA and had no history of neurological, respiratory, laryngeal, speech and voice disorders, except those associated with Parkinson's disease. In order to make the effects of the disease more discernible, patients were recorded in two separate pharmacological states. The first recording was made in the morning after L-DOPA withdrawal of at least 12 h (OFF-DOPA condition). A second recording was made later in the day, after a minimum of 1.5 h after taking L-DOPA (ON-DOPA condition). The dosage of L-DOPA is specific to each patient. Before registration, each patient's motor disability was assessed by a neurologist using the Unified Parkinson's Disease Rating Scale (UPDRS), in particular the severity of dysarthria as defined in item 18 [15]. Six control speakers matched by age and gender were also analyzed in this study. These subjects were selected in three age groups (50–60 years, 60–70 years, 70–80 years) in order to observe the variations in intraoral pressure in different age groups. Parkinsonian patients also had to have different disease durations and different UPDRS score evolutions in ON-DOPA and OFF-DOPA conditions in order to analyze the effect of L-DOPA treatment. The list of subjects is given in Table 1. In this study, we chose to work on a limited number of subjects be- cause we wanted to explore the singular characteristics of each subject. Indeed, we believe that it is necessary to compare one by one the Parkinsonian subjects to the control subjects in order to establish a robust model and to define the common, break and novelty areas. The aerodynamic reference data being limited for both pathological and healthy subjects, we believe that it is necessary to carry out a detailed study in order to identify an aerodynamic production profile. Undoubtedly, the results presented in this study will have to be verified on a larger scale.

Table 1. Characteristics of each patient and reference subject. Motor disorders are assessed using the Unified Parkinson's Disease Rating Scale (UPDRS). The degree of severity of dysarthria is defined with item 18: 0: normal speech; 1: slight loss of expression and voice volume and slight difficulty in diction; 2: monotonous, sub-articulated but intelligible, moderately de- graded; 3: markedly degraded, difficult to understand; 4: unintelligible.

Patient	Gender	Age	Disease duration	Total motor score (UPDRS)		Speech score (UPDRS)		Ctrl	Age
				ON	OFF	ON	OFF		
67	M	56	7	14	38	0	1	1785	51
610	M	69	16	13	36	1	2	1866	63
12	M	74	9	9	40	1	2	160	74
226	F	59	12	5	20	0	2	796	67
598	F	69	8	12, 5	39, 5	0,5	1, 5	1613	71
33	F	75	16	22, 5	35	1,5	1, 5	2374	77

2.2   Recording Methods

The experimental procedure follows the same conditions as presented in [8], acoustic and physiological data are recorded with the EVA workstation [16], which was designed to record and measure sound waves, pitch, SPL intensity, airflow, and pressure, for the evaluation of speech production. Multi-parametric data are recorded us- ing SESANE software (Software Environment for Speech ANalysis and Evaluation[1]). Oral airflow is measured with a flow meter based on a resistive grid (pneumotachograph principle) with a small dead volume and specific linearization for the inhaled and exhaled airflow [17]. A soft silicone rubber mask, pressed against the speaker's face prevents air leakage, without hindering articulatory movements. Subglottal pressure is estimated with the airway interrupted method [18] using a PVC probe located in the

---

[1] http://www.sqlab.fr.

subject's mouth and connected to the pressure sensor de- vice of the workstation while the subject is instructed to pronounce consecutive ad- hoc sentences ("*papa ne m'a pas parlé de beau papa*") at normal pitch, rate and loudness. During the occlusion of [p], the lips are closed, the glottis is opened, and the vocal tract can be considered as a single air volume from the lungs to the lips: pressure in the oral cavity is the same as in the sub-glottal cavity [22].

Intensity (RMS) was measured from the signal recorded with a high fidelity microphone placed on the transducers. The mouth was kept at a 4 cm constant distance from the microphone because the subject's cheek was in contact with the silicone mouthpiece.

2.3 Segmentation and Measurements

Subjects were asked to repeat the phrase "*Papa ne m'a pas parlé de beau papa*" eleven times at a constant rate, with a breath-hold between each repetition. We chose to analyze all the [p] in the sentence except the first one because it is usually mispronounced and barely sketched by the patients, which prevents correct detection of borders. The data were processed by the same annotator on the Phonedit software, specifically adapted to the study of aerodynamic parameters, to manually segment the consonants.

In order to achieve a homogeneous segmentation based on the same criteria for all subjects, we relied on Gracco's et al. [19] study, following the work by Müller and Brown [20], proposing an aerodynamic analysis of the production of stop consonants in Parkinson's disease (e.g., Fig. 1). In this study, Gracco et al. [19] distinguish three successive phases during the production of stop consonants; the closing phase during which the occlusion is established, the holding phase of occlusion during which the articulators remain in the closed position, and the opening phase during which the occlusion is released. The observation of the oral airflow rate (Oaf) and the intra-oral pressure (Po) makes possible to delimit these three phases. In fact, during the closing phase, Po increases behind the occlusion that is being set up and the oral airflow gradually decreases until it reaches the zero value when the occlusion is achieved. We have therefore positioned the start boundary (Condition A) at the moment when the oral airflow is approaching zero, attesting to good labial occlusion (e.g., Fig. 2). However, this labial occlusion is not always achieved in Parkinson's patients. Indeed, the weakening of the occlusion may result in the loss of features such as occlusion and burst (21). In absence of occlusion, we had to look for a segmentation method which could be applied to all subjects and which is constant in order to obtain homogeneous segmentation. To do this, we relied on the acoustic intensity curve, which proved to be very reliable in accurately marking the boundaries of occlusion and relaxation in Parkinson's subjects. We based our work on the following criteria: (1) The setting of the constrictions triggers a complete occlusion or a strong slowdown (narrow constriction) of the airflow and provokes an increase in the intra-oral pressure (Po) behind the constriction. An acoustic consequence of these constrictions is the abrupt decrease of the intensity of the signal. (2) When the constriction is released, there is a rapid decrease in intra-oral pressure and an increase in oral airflow. The acoustic consequence of relaxation is a rapid increase in the intensity of the acoustic signal (e.g., Fig. 3).

Figure 2 corresponds to the production of the logatome [papa] by the female patient 33 aged 75 years and having Parkinson's disease for 16 years at the time of recording (e.g., Table 1). This patient obtained a UPDRS score of 1.5 for the speech item in the OFF-DOPA condition. By observing the intra-oral pressure curves, oral airflow and intensity, it can be seen that, at the time of the closure phase, there is in- deed a progressive increase in intra-oral pressure with a simultaneous decrease in oral airflow which eventually reaches zero. This patient therefore manages to achieve the labial occlusion that can be identified by the flow curve. At the time of occlusion, when the oral airflow rate is at zero, an abrupt drop in intensity is observed. We there- fore have two clues for this subject allowing us to position the start boundary in order to extract the intra-oral pressure value, which here is 3,764 hPa (1.2 hPa = 1 CmH2O). The production of this subject is comparable to that of a healthy subject (e.g., Fig. 5). On the other hand, if we look at the production of the female subject 226 aged 59 years and having Parkinson's disease for 12 years, the boundaries are more difficult to detect (e.g., Fig. 3). This patient obtained a UPDRS OFF-DOPA score of 2 for the speech item, and her speech was therefore assessed by the neurologist as more degraded than that of subject 33. This difference is perceptible on the oral airflow curve because it is observed that lip occlusion is not complete. Moreover, the burst is not identifiable on the acoustic signal. In the absence of cues to precisely delimit the boundaries, we based ourselves for this subject on the intensity curve using the criteria defined above.

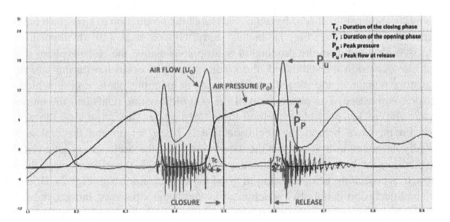

Fig. 1. Po and Oaf curves during the production of [p] from the Speech aerodynamics database [26], replicating Gracco et al. 1992 [19]. Tc = duration of the occlusion phase, Tr = duration of the release phase, Pp = peak intra-oral pressure, Pu = peak airflow at the time of release.

During holding phase of the occlusion, in which the articulators are held in the closed position, Po increases until it reaches a maximum value. When Po curve reaches a kind of plateau at the end of this rising phase and before the onset of the fall, the pressure peak (Condition B) is reached. We chose to extract the intra-oral pressure peak because it provides an identical reference point for all subjects, especially for those who do not make bursts when the occlusion of [p] is released. In addition, it provides an estimated of subglottal pressure value. Giovanni et al. [22] have shown that sub-glottal and intra-oral pressure have comparable values, when compared at intra-oral pressure peak, for voiceless bilabial consonants. Figure 5 clearly shows these three phases (rise, plateau and fall) of intra-oral pressure for a healthy subject. The measurements of the intra-oral pressure peaks therefore allow an estimation of the value of the subglottal pressure in Parkinson's patients Fig. (4).

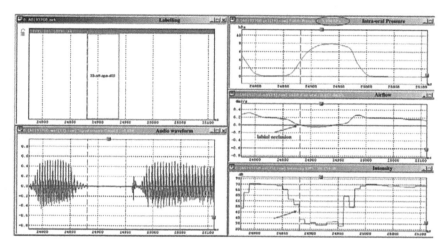

Fig. 2. At the top left the labeling window, at the bottom left the audio signal. On the right, the intra-oral pressure (Po), the oral air flow rate (Oaf) and the intensity curves when the patient labelled 33 pronounces the logatome [papa] in OFF-DOPA condition. The dotted red line is positioned at the time of the labial occlusion corresponding to condition A.

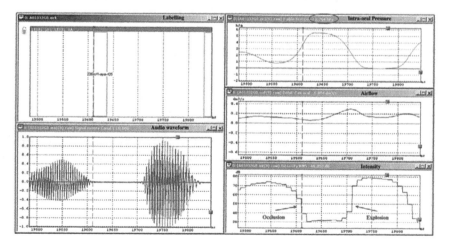

Fig. 3. At the top left the labeling window, at the bottom left the audio signal. On the right, the intra-oral pressure (Po), the oral air flow rate (Oaf) and the intensity curves when the patient labelled 226 pronounces the logatome [papa] in OFF-DOPA condition. The dotted red line is positioned at the time of occlusion that corresponds to condition A. The arrows indicate the occlusion and burst phases identified with the intensity curve.

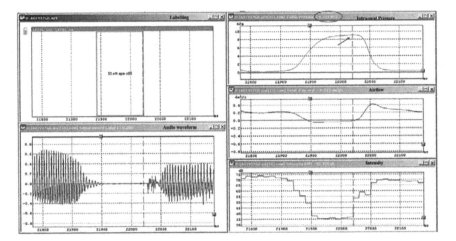

Fig. 4. At the top left the labeling window, at the bottom left the audio signal. On the right, the intra-oral pressure (Po), the oral air flow rate (Oaf) and the intensity curves when the patient labelled 33 pronounces the logatome [papa] in OFF-DOPA condition. The dotted red line is positioned at the time of the intra-oral pressure peak that corresponds to condition B.

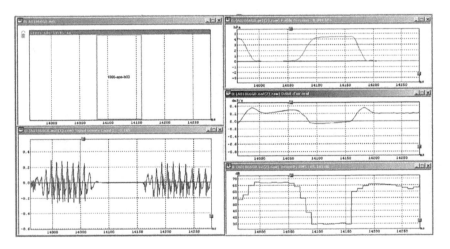

Fig. 5. At the top left the labeling window, at the bottom left the audio signal. On the right, the intra-oral pressure, oral airflow and intensity when control subject 1866 pronounces [papa].

3   Results

Figure 6 and 7 show the evolution of intra-oral pressure at 5 measurement points corresponding to the different positions of the bilabial consonant [p] in the sentence *"papa ne m'a pas parlé de beau papa"* except for the first [p]. Intra-oral pressure measurements were extracted at the time of occlusion (Condition A) and at the time of the intra-oral pressure peak (Condition B). Intra-oral pressure constitute the central point of our analysis because it is an extremely robust parameter for understanding the characteristics of French stop consonants. Indeed, as soon as there is an alteration of the constrictions or a movement of an articulator, the information is encoded in the intra-oral pressure measurements. Our objective is to understand how this parameter varies at different measurement points according to several controlled constraints (sex, age, duration of the disease, pharmacological status of patients, degree of severity of dysarthria) for patients in ON-DOPA and OFF-DOPA conditions. We will com- pare these results with those obtained for control subjects.

Tables 3 and 4 present the results of the statistical treatments of male (e.g., Table 3) and female subjects (e.g., Table 4). Subjects were instructed to repeat the phrase *"Papa ne m'a pas parlé de beau papa"* eleven times at a constant rate. Unfortunately, we could not take into account the eleven repetitions for the analysis because for some patients the data were incomplete: difficulties in completing the sentence, pronunciation error, [p] not pronounced by the subjects in some segments, [p] made as fricatives. In order to obtain the same number of measurements, we kept five sentences per subject. For all subjects, we averaged the Po values for the five sentences at points p2, p3, p4, p5 and p6 in condition A and B. For the statistical analyses, we observed the distribution of the data in order to see if it was possible to apply a Stu- dent's t-test. We chose to apply the Student t-test comparing two independent (un- paired) sample groups. Before applying this test, we verified that the data meet two conditions: (1) the sampling distribution follows a normal distribution, (2) the variances of the two groups are equal. Knowing that our samples to be compared have a sample size smaller than 30 (N = 5), we applied the Shapiro-Wilk normality test. Then, we compared the variances of the two groups. We found that the variances were significantly different. We therefore applied a Welch test which is an adaptation of Stu- dent's t-test, as the two groups followed a normal distribution with unequal variances. We defined our statistical comparisons as follows: the measures of Po represented the numerical factor; the group (CTRL, ON, OFF), the position of the consonant/p/in the sentences produced (P2, P3, P4, P5 and P6), the condition (A, B) and the subject (patients, CTRL) were the four factors of variability. A p-value of less than 0.05 was used as the statistical significance threshold.

Tables 2 and 5 show the decrease percentage of the Po curve from point 2 to point 6 for male and female subjects in the ON and OFF conditions and for control subjects during the production of the sentences *"Papa ne m'a pas parlé de beau papa"*.

3.1   Male Subjects

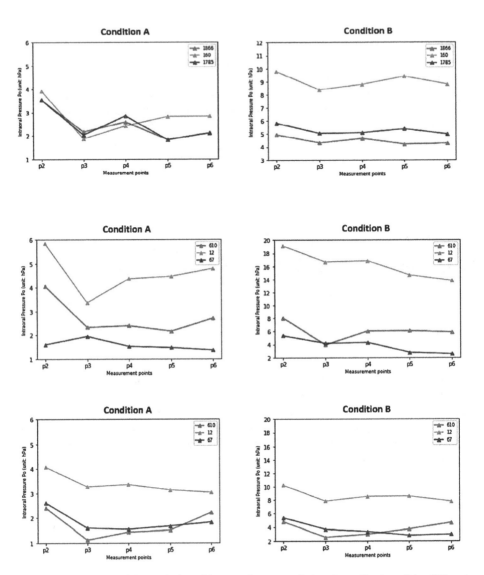

Fig. 6. Visualization of the evolution of intra-oral pressure during the realization of the different [p] produced in the sentence "*papa ne m'a pas parlé de beau papa*". At the top the curves of healthy male subjects, in the middle those of Parkinsonian subjects in ON-DOPA condition and at the bottom those of Parkinsonian subjects in OFF-DOPA condition. On the left, the results in condition A and on the right the results in condition B

Table 2. Tendencies for decrease of Po measurements for ON, OFF and CTRL groups.

	Difference (P2-P6)	Percentage of decrease ([P2–P6]/P2) * 100
12-OFF	2,42	−23.67%
12-ON	5.34	−27.91%
160 CTRL	0.98	−10,02%
610-OFF	0.14	−2.92%
610-ON	2.16	−26.83%
1866-CTRL	0.66	−13.38%
67-OFF	2.45	−45.45%
67-ON	2.81	−52.62%
1785-CTRL	0.84	−14.43%

Table 3. Summary of the measurements and statistical analysis performed for healthy male subjects (ctrl) and Parkinsonian subjects in ON-DOPA and OFF-DOPA condition. For each subject we illustrate the mean of intra-oral pressure (Po) in condition A (start) and in condition B (peak) as well as T-test values ($* p < .05; ** p < .01; *** p < .001$).

	P2		P3		P4		P5		P6	
	A	B	A	B	A	B	A	B	A	B
12-off	4.07	10.22	3.27	7.84	3.36	8.54	3.13	8.57	3.03	7.80
12-on	5.85	19.13	3.36	16.66	4.36	16.82	4.46	14.65	4.79	13.79
160-ctrl	3.92	9.78	1.87	8.37	2.42	8.78	2.81	9.39	2.82	8.80
p-value ON/OFF	0.04 *	1.074e−07 ***	0.93	0.0003 ***	0.27	0.0008 ***	0.05	0.007 **	0.006 **	2.126e−05 ***
p-value CTRL/ON	0.10	1.756e−06 ***	0.20	0.0005 ***	0.07	0.001 **	0.03 *	0.009 **	0.002 **	7.794e−05 ***
p-value CTRL/OFF	0.89	0.50	0.01 *	0.09	0.03 *	0.44	0.50	0.06	0.68	0.04 *
610-off	2.41	4.79	1.11	2.51	1.42	2.95	1.50	3.71	2.21	4.65
610-on	4.06	8.05	2.32	3.95	2.39	6.06	2.15	6.09	2.69	5.89
1866-ctrl	3.52	4.93	2.16	4.31	2.58	4.65	1.82	4.21	2.11	4.27
p-value ON/OFF	0.009 **	0.0002 ***	0.08	0.08	0.02 *	0.0005 ***	0.05	0.001 **	0.24	0.009 **
p-value CTRL/ON	0.32	0.0001 ***	0.79	0.57	0.50	0.0009 ***	0.35	0.008 **	0.13	0.003 **
p-value CTRL/OFF	0.02 *	0.75	0.04 *	0.009 **	0.004 **	0.01 *	0.25	0.35	0.75	0.23
67-off	2.61	5.39	1.59	3.68	1.54	3.34	1.67	2.78	1.82	2.94
67-on	1.60	5.34	1.94	4.19	1.52	4.31	1.47	2.76	1.36	2.53
1785-ctrl	3.53	5.82	2.03	5.04	2.84	5.09	1.82	5.38	2.11	4.98
p-value ON/OFF	0.04 *	0.94	0.40	0.58	0.95	0.26	0.64	0.97	0.26	0.59
p-value CTRL/ON	0.002 **	0.27	0.81	0.29	0.01 *	0.28	0.39	0.02 *	0.02 *	0.02 *
p-value CTRL/OFF	0.08	0.40	0.25	0.07	0.01 *	0.02 *	0.76	0.0007 ***	0.45	0.0008 ***

3.2   Female Subjects

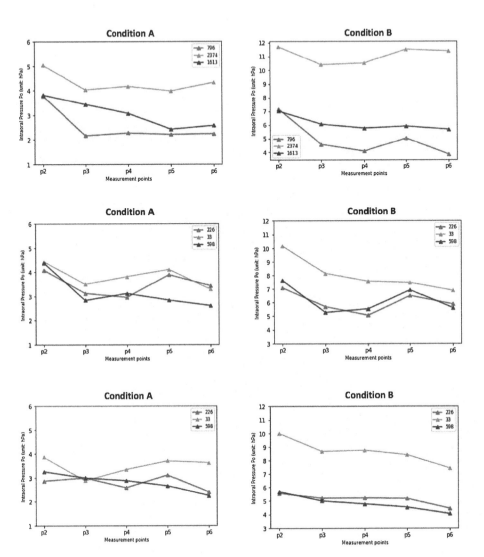

Fig. 7. Visualization of the evolution of intra-oral pressure during the realization of the different [p] produced in the sentence "*papa ne m'a pas parlé de beau papa*". At the top the curves of healthy male subjects, in the middle those of Parkinsonian subjects in ON-DOPA condition and at the bottom those of Parkinsonian subjects in OFF-DOPA condition. On the left, the results in condition A and on the right the results in condition B.

Table 4. Summary of the measurements and statistical analysis performed for healthy male subjects (ctrl) and Parkinsonian subjects in ON-DOPA and OFF-DOPA condition. For each subject we illustrate the mean of intra-oral pressure (Po) in condition A (start) and in condition B (peak) as well as T-test values ($* p < .05$; $** p < .01$; $*** p < .001$).

	P2		P3		P4		P5		P6	
	A	B	A	B	A	B	A	B	A	B
226-off	2.86	5.56	2.98	5.21	2.57	5.22	3.10	5.17	2.39	4.44
226-on	4.07	7.08	3.11	5.69	2.94	5.05	3.88	6.49	3.43	5.87
796-ctrl	3.77	7.17	2.16	4.58	2.27	4.08	2.21	5.04	2.24	3.86
p-value ON/OFF	0.05	0.008 **	0.68	0.04 *	0.38	0.70	0.07	3.937e−05 ***	0.05	2.27e−05 ***
p-value CTRL/ON	0.62	0.80	0.02 *	0.001 **	0.011 *	0.05	0.001 *	0.03 *	0.03 *	0.003 **
p-value CTRL/OFF	0.08	0.008 **	0.009 **	0.0001 ***	0.35	0.002 **	0.02 *	0.80	0.60	0.23
33-off	3.85	9.98	2.87	8.66	3.34	8.74	3.69	8.40	3.62	7.42
33-on	4.43	10.16	3.49	8.13	3.81	7.56	4.10	7.45	3.28	6.87
Ctrl-2374	5.03	11.71	4.03	10.40	4.16	10.52	3.97	11.53	4.32	11.46
p-value ON/OFF	0.39	0.80	0.39	0.26	0.41	0.19	0.53	0.18	0.47	0.19
p-value CTRL/ON	0.34	0.01 *	0.42	0.001 **	0.55	0.01 *	0.87	0.0002 ***	0.30	0.001 **
p-value CTRL/OFF	0.11	0.03 *	0.07	0.01 *	0.22	4.904e−05 ***	0.69	0.0002 ***	0.46	0.003 **
598-off	3.25	5.68	2.98	5.00	2.87	4.77	2.65	4.53	2.24	4.05
598-on	4.37	7.63	2.82	5.26	3.11	5.53	2.83	6.91	2.60	5.60
1613-ctrl	3.81	7.02	3.43	6.06	3.07	5.78	2.42	5.92	2.57	5.69
p-value ON/OFF	0.07	0.01 *	0.68	0.67	0.55	0.17	0.66	0.01 *	0.36	0.005 **
p-value CTRL/ON	0.52	0.27	0.17	0.20	0.92	0.64	0.19	0.18	0.96	0.73
p-value CTRL/OFF	0.48	0.02 *	0.12	0.02 *	0.66	0.02 *	0.50	0.04 *	0.63	0.003 **

Table 5. Tendencies for decrease of Po measurements for ON, OFF and CTRL groups.

	Difference (P2–P6)	Percentage of decrease ([P2–P6]/P2)*100
226-OFF	1.12	−20.14%
226-ON	1.21	−17.09%
796-CTRL	3.31	−46%
33-OFF	2.56	−25.65%
33-ON	3.29	−32.38%
2374-CTRL	0.31	−2.64%
598-OFF	1.63	−28.69%
598-ON	2.03	−26.60%
1613-CTRL	1.33	−18.94%

4 Discussion

Po measurements are found to be higher in the ON-DOPA condition compared to the OFF-DOPA condition. This increase is perceptible in both segmentation conditions but it is clearly more marked in condition B at the Po peak. This result is expected because the measurements taken in condition B correspond to the end of the rise of Po when it reaches its maximum value. We will therefore essentially study the results obtained under condition B. Subject 12 is the one with the largest increase of Po in the ON-DOPA condition. Indeed, the mean difference between the two conditions (ON- OFF) is around 7.6 hPa and is statistically highly significant at all measurement points. A significant improvement of Po is also observed for subject 610 at p2, p4 and p6. This increase is smaller than the one observed for subject 12 with a mean difference of 2.3 hPa. On the contrary, for subject 67, no significant difference was observed between the two conditions. However, it can be seen that Po averages are generally higher when patient 67 is in the OFF-DOPA condition, unlike the other patients (e.g., Table 3). This difference could be due to the fact that patient 67 was assessed by the neurologist as having less speech impairment with a score of 0 in the ON-DOPA condition and a score of 1 in the OFF-DOPA condition, whereas subjects 67 and 610 obtained a score of 1 in the ON-DOPA condition and a score of 2 in the OFF-DOPA condition. Score 1 corresponds to a slight loss of expression and voice volume with a slight difficulty in diction while score 2 corresponds to monotonous, sub-articulated and moderately degraded but intelligible speech (e.g., Table 1). Therefore, it seems that dopaminergic treatment has a greater impact on the improvement of Po when the patient has a more degraded speech in the OFF-DOPA condition because this degradation is induced by a dysfunction of the respiratory musculature (random alteration of the expiratory air flow, alteration of the quantity of air necessary for the vibration of vocal folds) partly responsible of dysarthria [23]. The results obtained for female subjects seem to reinforce this hypothesis (e.g., Table 4). Indeed, the female patient 226 is the one who obtains the highest increase of Po among the female subjects with a significant difference at all measurement points except p4. In fact, this patient was assessed to have the most degraded speech among female subjects with a score of 2, while other female patients scored 1.5 for the speech item in OFF condition. Nevertheless, there was an improvement in Po for patient 598 on p2, p5 and p6 even though it was less significant. On the other hand, there was no difference between the two conditions for patient 33. Dopaminergic treatment does not appear to be effective in improving this patient's speech impairment. This lack of difference reflects the scores given by the neurologist since this patient obtained a UPDRS score of 1.5 in both the ON and OFF conditions. Intraoral pressure measurements in ON and OFF condition are consistent with the neurologist's assessment. This result suggests that Po is an interesting parameter to consider that could complement the neurologist's assessment and provide an additional descriptor to predict the UPDRS score from speech signals. In order to confirm this result, we would like to conduct this study on a larger scale.

Patients 226, 12 and 610 were found to have higher Po values in ON condition than control subjects. This difference is statistically highly significant for subject 12 for all measurement points with a mean difference of 7 hPa. For subject 610, the same difference is significantly attested for all points except p3 and for subject 226 at p3, p5 and p6. This drug-induced overshoot phenomenon is promising as it shows that L-DOPA treatment can restore Po. These results differ from those obtained in the study by Sarr and Al. [8] on male patients with neurostimulation device where Po restoration took place only on the initial part of the phase with Po values in ON condition significantly lower than those of the control subjects. For subjects 598 and 67 there was no significant difference between the Po measurements for these subjects and their control subjects. The values obtained are nearly equivalent. This result is expected because patient 598 obtained a score of 0.5 in ON condition and subject 67 a score of 0. Subject 33 obtained lower Po values in ON condition compared to control subject with a significant difference in all points except p2. This is also an expected result because, as we have seen previously, there is no alteration or improvement of Po for this subject between the ON and OFF conditions for which he obtained a score of 1.5. Once again, we see that there is a statistical relationship between Po and UPDRS scores.

The observation of the curves as well as of the Po averages at different measurement points reflects that intra-oral pressure seems to be higher at the beginning of production but that it tends to decrease over time. This phenomenon is the declination of the subglottic pressure because, as a reminder, during the holding phase of the voiceless stop consonant during the pressure peak, the subglottic pressure is usually equal to the intra-oral pressure. The decline in subglottic pressure can be explained as follows [24]: normally, to sustain the energy necessary for speech, the diminution of the lung volume needs to be compensated by the contribution of thoracic and abdominal muscles, in addition to the normal lung recoil forces. This is for maintaining a sufficient subglottic pressure for speech and to compensate for this decrease in air volume during expiration [24]. As the volume decreases, the subglottic pressure decreases mechanically. The decline in subglottic pressure occurs because this mechanism is not fully compensated by the muscles controlling expiration. As the subglottic pressure decreases, the laryngeal frequency that depends on it drops. In order to study this phenomenon, we calculated the decrease percentage of the Po curve from point 2 to point 6 for male and female subjects in the ON and OFF conditions and for control subjects (e.g., Table 2 and 5).

It can be seen that the drop of Po is greater in the ON condition than in the OFF condition. These results are similar to those obtained by Sarr et al. [11] on male patients with a neurostimulation device. They had hypothesized that the drop of Po was greater in ON than in OFF because of a "floor effect": patients in OFF condition start from a lower Po level at the beginning; their margin of decrease is then necessarily narrower, the final "floor" level being substantially the same for both ON and OFF conditions. The opposite effect is observed for female subjects with a greater fall of Po in the OFF condition than in the ON condition except for subject 33 who has a greater fall in the ON condition than in the OFF condition. In fact, from points p2 to p4 the results are similar to those obtained for the male subjects and for the female subject 33 with a greater emphasis at the beginning of production in ON condition which translates into a greater respiratory effort achievable thanks to the dopaminergic treatment which has the consequence of increasing the available energy and obtaining a greater increase of Po in ON than in OFF. However, at the end of the phase there is an emphasis realized by both subjects on the realization of the 5th [p] which has the consequence of reducing the declination.

In this study, intraoral pressure was found to be higher for older subjects. Indeed, subject 12 is the oldest male subject (74 years old). However, we find that he obtains higher Po values compared to other younger males. If we look at the results obtained for his control subject (160) of the same age, we can see that he also has a higher Po. The same pattern is observed for female subjects. Indeed, the female patient 33 (75 years old) and her control subject (77 years old) obtain higher Po values than younger subjects. This result seems surprising, but it could be explained by a reduction in respiratory capacity, linked to the age of the patients and controls subjects. Indeed, Parkinson's disease generally manifests itself in elderly people who may experience a functional decline of the disease that is superimposed on functional changes in the larynx with aging. As we get older, we see a decrease in the elasticity of the lungs, although this is quite variable depending on the individual [25]. This reduction in the elasticity of the lungs may result in an increase in the value of the pressure measured in the lung volume. In our data, the measured pressure (Po) is that of the volume between the lips, which are normally closed, and the lungs since the glottis is open or the realization of [p]. This result is consistent with the study by Higgins et al. [27] in which older healthy subjects had significantly higher subglottic pressure values than younger healthy subjects. Few aerodynamic studies report aero- dynamic values in elderly people with Parkinson's disease relative to their healthy peers. This tells us that it is important to consider the age variable in the aerodynamic analysis of Parkinson's patients because the effects of normal aging on speech behaviour could be confused with those of laryngeal disease.

5   Conclusions

In this study, we presented our work on the contribution of automatic speech processing tools in the context of dysarthric speech, with the ultimate aim of highlighting the relevance of selected parameters that are little exploited in automatic detection and prediction approaches. In the first part, an innovative segmentation method based on intensity measurement was presented. This method has proved to be relevant for the segmentation of stop consonants because it allows relying on stable and easily detectable clues despite pathological speech with no occlusion or burst. A future goal would be to exploit RMS intensity measurements to study the correlation between subglottic pressure and intensity. In the second part of the study, we analyzed the variations in intra-oral pressure. We examined whether it reflected or provided information on the severity of Parkinson's disease symptoms, as defined by the Unified Parkinson's Disease Rating Scale (UPDRS) standard clinical reference scale. Despite the wide inter-pathological variability observed in dysarthric speech, intraoral pressure was found to be a potential indicator or grading index that could complement the neurologist's assessment and be included in the diagnostic and therapeutic control package for the neurologist. We wish to conduct this study on a larger scale to confirm the correlation between intra-oral pressure and UPDRS scores.

References

1. Kegl, J., Cohen, H., Poizner, H.: Articulatory consequences of Parkinson's disease: perspectives from two modalities. Brain Cogn. **40**, 355–386 (1999)
2. Walsh, B., Basic, A.: Parameters of articulatory movements and acoustics in individuals with parkinson's disease. Mov. Disord. **27**, 843–850 (2012)
3. Moro-Velazquez, L., et al.: Phonetic relevance and phonemic grouping of speech in the automatic detection of Parkinson's disease. Sci. Rep. **9**(1), 1–16 (2019)
4. Darley, F.L., Aronson, A.E., Brown, J.R.: Differential diagnostic patterns of dysarthria. J. Speech Hear. Res. **12**, 246–269 (1969)
5. Gentil, M., Pollak, P., et Perret, J.: La dysarthrie parkinsonienne. Revue Neurologique, Mason, Paris 151-2:105–112 (1995)
6. Ho, A.K., Bradshaw, J.L., Cunnington, R., Phillips, J.G., Iansek, R.: Sequence heterogeneity in parkinsonian speech. Brain Lang. **64**, 122–145 (1998)
7. Baken, R.J., Orlikoff, R.F.: Clinical Measurement of Speech and Voice. Singular, San Diego (2000)
8. Ghio, A., et al.: How to manage sound, physiological and clinical data of 2500 dysphonic and dysarthric speakers? Speech Commun. **54**(5), 664–679 (2012)
9. Duez, D.: Syllable structure, syllable duration and final lengthening in Parkinsonian French speech. J. Multilingual Comm. Disord. **4**(1), 45–57 (2006)
10. Duez, D., Legou, T., Viallet, F.: Final lengthening in Parkinsonian French speech: effects of position in phrase on the duration of CV syllables and speech segments. Clin. Linguist. Phon. **23**(11), 781–793 (2009)
11. Sarr, M.M., et al.: Contribution de la mesure de la pression intra-orale pour la compréhension des troubles de la coordination pneumophonique dans la dysarthrie parkinsonienne. Rev. Neurol. **165**(12), 1055–1061 (2009)
12. Viallet, F., Jankowski, L., Purson, A., Teston, B.: Dopa effects on laryngeal dysfunction in Parkinson's disease: an acoustic and aerodynamic study abstract. Mov. Disord. **19**(S9), S237 (2004)
13. Viallet, F., Teston, B., Jankowski, L., Purson, A., Peragut, J., Regis, J., Witjas, T.: Effects of pharmacological versus electrophysiological treatments on Parkinsonian dysprosody, pp. 679–682. Proc. Speech Prosody. Aix-en-Provence, France (2002)
14. Viallet, F., Teston, B.: Objective evaluation of dysphonia: acoustic and aerodynamic methods. Proc. Around Dysphasia, Dysarthria, Dysphonia, 53–55 (2003)
15. Fahn, S., Marsden, G., Goldstein, M., Caline, D.: Recent Developments in Parkinson's disease (Vol 2). Macmillian Healthcare Information, Florham Park, NJ (1987)
16. Teston, B., Galindo, B.: A diagnosis of rehabilitation aid workstation for speech and voice pathologies. In: Proceedings of European Conference on Speech Communication and Technology (Eurospeech), pp. 1883–1886 (1995)
17. Ghio, A., Teston, B., Evaluation of the acoustic and aerodynamic constraints of a pneumotachograph for speech and voice studies. In: International Conference on Voice Physiology and Biomecanics, Marseille, France, 18–20 August, pp. 55–58 (2004)
18. Smitheran, J.R., Hixon, T.J.: A clinical method for estimating laryngeal airway resistance during vowel production. J. Speech Hear. Disord. **46**, 138–146 (1981)
19. Gracco, L.C, Gracco, V.L., Löfqvist, A., Marek, K.: An aerodynamic evaluation of Parkinsonian dysarthria: laryngeal and supralaryngeal manifestations. Haskins Laboratories Status Rep. Speech Res. SR-111/112:103–110 (1992)

20. Müller, E.M., Brown, W.S.: Variations in the supraglottal air pressure waveform and their articulatory interpretation. Speech and Language: Advances in Basic Research and Practice, vol. 4. Academic Press, New York (1980)

21. Duez, D.: On spontaneous French speech: aspects of the reduction and contextual assimilation of intervocalic voiced plosives in spontaneous French speech. J. Phonetics **23**, 407–427 (1995)

22. Giovanni, A., Demolin, D., Heim, C., Triglia, J.M.: Estimated subglottic pressure in normal and dysphonic subjects. Ann Otol Rhinol Laryngol **109**, 500–504 (2000)

23. Murdoch, B.E., Chenery, H.J., Bowler, S., Ingram, J.C.: Respiratory function in Parkinson's subjects exhibiting a perceptible speech deficit a kinematic and spirometric analysis. J Speech Hear Disord. **54**(4), 610–626 (1989)

24. Ladefoged, P.: Three Areas of Experimental Phonetics. Oxford University Press, London (1967)

25. Bouhuys, A.: The Physiology of Breathing: A Textbook for Medical Students. Grune & Stratton, New-York (1977)

26. Demolin, D., Hassid, S., Ponchard, C., Yu, S., Trouville, R.: Speech aerodynamics database. hal-02503114 (2019)

27. Higgins, M.B., Saxman, J.H.: A comparison of selected phonatory behaviors of healthy aged and young adults. J. Speech Hear. Res. **34**(5), 1000–1010 (1991)

Approaches to Evaluate Parkinsonian Speech Using Artificial Models

J. I. Godino-Llorente[1(✉)] , L. Moro-Velázquez[2] ,
J. A. Gómez-García[1] , Jeung-Yoon Choi[3], N. Dehak[2] ,
and S. Shattuck-Hufnagel[3]

[1] Theory and Communications Department, Universidad Politécnica de Madrid,
C/ Nikola Tesla s/n, 28031 Madrid, Spain
ignacio.godino@upm.es
[2] Center for Language and Speech Processing, Johns Hopkins University,
3400 North Charles Street, Baltimore, MD 21218-2680, USA
[3] Speech Communication Group, Massachusetts Institute of Technology,
50 Vassar St., Cambridge, MA 02139-4307, USA

Abstract. Our preliminary data and experiments show the potentiality of the artificial intelligence techniques to identify Parkinson's disease and to assess its extent using the information extracted from the speech. Our conclusions are based on several prospective studies with different corpora of parkinsonian and control subjects modelled following different approaches, mainly grounded on articulatory aspects of the speech and on the use of probabilistic generative models inspired in those used in the field of speaker recognition. Results obtained are consistent among the different approaches and corpora, providing detection accuracies over 85%. This chapter compiles and compares the approaches we followed and the results we obtained in the last few years, and discusses some key aspects for future research in the field.

The goal is not only to demonstrate the potentiality of the artificial intelligence techniques used, but also to extract from them significant knowledge that might be of interest for our understanding of the effects of the disease on the speech. To this respect a phonemic analysis based on the automatic techniques developed is carried out, suggesting important cues about the acoustic units that are more affected by the disease.

Keywords: Parkinson's Disease · Speech · Hypokinetic dysarthria · Automatic detection · Kinematic analysis · Phonemic analysis

1 Introduction

Early diagnosis and treatment of idiopathic Parkinson's Disease (PD) are vital to alleviate the effects of the disease. However, despite the efforts, to date there are not early and non-invasive robust markers. Some of these efforts are focused in the analysis of certain biometric patterns such as gait [1], speech [2], handwriting [3], through touchpad devices [4], and typing patterns [5]. The automatic analysis of the speech is an emerging field with potential to generate quantitative non-invasive biomarkers

J. I. Godino-Llorente (Ed.): AAPS 2019, CCIS 1295, pp. 77–99, 2020.
https://doi.org/10.1007/978-3-030-65654-6_5

derived from clinical tests, and pioneering studies are identifying that the speech is affected even in the pre-clinical phase [6]. Thus, our goal is to identify reliable biomarkers based on digital signal processing and artificial intelligence techniques extracted from the speech, but gaining new knowledge from the artificial models developed. This would open the possibility to design non-invasive automatic detection and screening systems, enabling a change of paradigm in early PD monitoring and in its differential evaluation with respect to other atypical parkinsonisms. In this context, our focus is on the identification of biomarkers directly or indirectly linked with articulatory and kinetic aspects of the speech, under the assumption that they are highly correlated with the existing motor symptoms. The long term goal will be to gain new knowledge about the interaction among speech and PD, which could be used for diagnosis, assessment, and rehabilitation purposes, especially in the early stages.

Despite the amount of research in the field, there is still room for developing new knowledge, not only about the characteristics of the speech of people affected with PD, but also about its correlation with the extent of the disease. Automatic systems to evaluate and assess the disease will take advantage of the new knowledge generated in the field to make more accurate and robust systems.

This chapter reports some of the most significant conclusions and results obtained to date in the framework of the projects: "*Objective Evaluation of Parkinson Disease and other Parkinsonisms*", funded by MISTI MIT International Science and Technology Initiatives; and "*Biomarkers for the diagnosis and assessment of Parkinson's Disease based on multimodal studies of speech and oculographic signals* (DPI2017-83405-R1)", funded by the Spanish Ministry of Economy and Competitiveness.

1.1   State of the Art

PD affects the cells producing dopamine in the brain, leading to dysfunctions of the basal ganglia, and manifesting motoric symptoms. Symptoms include, among others, reduced range of motion, postural instability, bradykinesia, and muscle tremor. Despite the advances and efforts, due to the overlapping of clinical signs with other diseases, the diagnosis of PD usually has a delay of 1 to 5 yr (with an average of 2,9 yr), and up to 19% takes more than 5 yr to get to the diagnosis [7]. After diagnosis, treatments can help relieve symptoms and to delay the neurodegeneration but, up to date, there is no cure. Thus an early diagnosis is essential, and the speech is one of these biomarkers requiring more research to evaluate its potentiality for this purpose.

From the early works in [8, 9], literature reports a large number of studies with the goal of characterizing the speech of parkinsonian people. Typically, PD is associated to a decrease of intelligibility in the spoken language due to impairments at phonatory, articulatory, prosodic and even at linguistic levels of the speech, leading to what is commonly known as hypokinetic dysarthria (HD) [10, 11]. HD, which is mainly linked with a decreased range of motion in the speech production mechanisms, is the primary factor contributing to the speech disorder in PD, being developed by 90% of the people during the course of the disease [12, 13]. Nevertheless some patients (10–20%) develop mixed hypokinetic-hyperkinetic dysarthria [14]. Hyperkinetic, in contrast, refers to involuntary movements of the speech production system due to basal ganglia control circuit pathology. These involuntary movements affect the speech mechanism in the form of dyskinesias that are related to long-term levodopa usage [15].

The dysarthrias secondary to PD mainly manifest at phonatory, articulatory and prosodic levels, and include a large set of symptoms, such as dysphonia (in the form of harshness and breathiness), tremor, hypernasality, imprecise consonants, repeated phonemes, reduced stress, monopitch, monoloudness, reduced overall loudness, short rushes of speech, short phrases, variable rate, overall increased rate, and inappropriate silences [10].

The aforementioned suggests that an automatic analysis of the speech might be useful to extract cues about the presence of the disease. However, despite the afore-mentioned, auditory-perceptual judgments are still the "gold standard" for guiding clinical dysarthria decisions in PD. But researchers started to develop tools for the automatic analysis of the speech of parkinsonian people. Roughly speaking, depending on the acoustic material and the artificial intelligence techniques used, the automatic approaches can be categorized according to the level addressed: phonatory, articulatory or prosodic.

To this respect, researchers have mainly placed the focus on the automatic analysis of phonatory aspects, since they are easy to measure from sustained vowels. The acoustic analysis in [16] using sustained vowels concluded that PD patients present differences in noise and tremor. However, the tremor of patients with PD does not always occur, being slow (3–7 Hz), present in no more than 55% of PD patients, and difficult to measure (i.e. requires long sustained phonations). On the other hand, although there are papers that show an increase in the mean fundamental frequency, jitter and shimmer [17], the literature suggests some controversy about the usefulness of phonation measures extracted from sustained vowels [18] to detect PD. Thus, results at phonatory level are constrained, on one hand, by the methods available in speech technology, and on the other by the limited discriminative information provided at this level. Consequently, the clinical reliability of most of the methods developed at phonatory level is being questioned by some researchers [19], although recent works have reported very good results [20, 21].

In any case, a more reliable approach and more correlated with the disease might be at articulatory level, since most significant disturbances appear at this level, being the next challenge in the automatic analysis of parkinsonian speech. Articulatory deficits manifest themselves as a reduction in amplitude, precision, speed and variability of the movements of the lips, jaw and tongue during articulation. In addition, patients with PD make inaccuracies in the production of consonants due to poor placement of the articulators. In this sense, the literature reports late incomplete occlusive consonants [22]. The inaccurate articulation of the end of the consonants usually results in low frequency frication noise that replaces the silences or gaps between some allophones as a consequence of the reduction of the closure [23]. Likewise, the variability of the voice onset time for vocal and consonant stops is also an indicator of the presence of PD [24].

Thanks to the recent advances in speech technology we are in a good place to address the automatic detection of PD speech at this level. In this chapter we mainly focus on an automatic analysis of articulatory aspects of the speech. However, rather than developing systems for the automatic detection of PD, our interest stands more on applying artificial intelligence techniques to extract new knowledge that might be of interest to understand how the speech is affected by the disease.

This chapter is structured as follows: Sect. 2 is dedicated to present the speech corpora that were used for the experiments; Sect. 3 is dedicated to a kinematic analysis of the speech; Sect. 4 to a phonemic analysis, proposing techniques to study the relevance of different phonemic units; and, finally, Sect. 5 is dedicated to present the most significant conclusions and future directions.

2   Corpora

The experiments presented in this paper were carried out using two corpora of Spanish speakers. The first contains recordings of European Spanish speakers and the second the speech of Colombian Spanish speakers.

The first corpus, called *Neurovoz* was recorded with the collaboration of the neurology and otorhinolaryngology services at the Gregorio Marañón Hospital, in Madrid, Spain. It contains 47 patients with idiopathic PD and 32 control speakers, who were recorded in a controlled acoustic environment with mid-high quality equipment, at a comfortable speech Sound Pressure Level (SPL). Recording contains the spontaneous speech describing a picture, utterances of a Diadochokinetik (DDK) task (repetitions of the sequence /pa-ta-ka/), and six fixed sentences previously memorized by the speaker. Table 1 reports some demographic statistics of the corpus, and more details can be found in [25].

The second, called *GITA*, was recorded at the Clínica Noel, in Medellín, Colombia, and contains 50 patients with idiopathic PD and 50 control speakers, also recorded with mid-high quality equipment at a comfortable SPL and in a controlled acoustic environment. The corpus is balanced in age and sex. The recordings contain a DDK task (the rapid and repetitive uttering of /pa-ta-ka/), a monologue and six text-dependent tasks who were read by the speaker. Table 1 reports some demographic statistics of the corpus. Further details can be found in [26].

Table 1. Demographic statistics of *GITA* and *Neurovoz* corpora.

	GITA				Neurovoz			
	Female		Male		Female		Male	
	PD	HC	PD	HC	PD	HC	PD	HC
# Subjects	25	25	25	25	18	18	29	14
Mean age (yr)	60.7	61.4	61.6	60.5	70,9	68.4	71.9	66.6
Age, range (yr)	49–75	49–76	33–81	31–86	59–86	58–83	41–88	55–77
UPDRS average	37.6	–	37.7	-	18.2	–	7.4	–
H&Y average	2.2	–	2.3	-	2.3	–	2.3	–
yr since diagnosis	12.6	–	8.9	-	6.6	–	7.4	–

Apart from these two main corpora, two other were used to train background and/or auxiliary models: the *Albayzin* corpus [27], which is a phonetically balanced dataset, composed by a large number of utterances in European Spanish language and their transcriptions; and the *FisherSP* (Fisher Spanish) corpus [28], created by the Linguistic Data Consortium, which contains around 163 h of telephonic speech from 136 native Spanish language speakers from at least 20 countries.

3 Kinematic Analysis

The kinematic analysis stands on the hypothesis that the mechanisms to control the articulators in patients with PD produce smoother, slower and less extended movements than in control speakers. This means that the distance travelled by the articulators is less than expected, the time required to change their position is larger, and the forces involved in the control system are lower or are less stable in the short term. Thus, in view of the quadratic relationship between the kinetic energy and velocity, and the direct relationship between force and acceleration, an indirect way to measure the stated effects is by using the speed and acceleration of different magnitudes which are supposed to be correlated with the movements.

Having this in mind we developed two different approaches. The first one is based on state of the art cepstral and linear parameterization approaches combined with speaker verifications techniques [29], whereas the second evaluates the velocity and acceleration of the envelope as an indirect measurement of the movements of the articulators [30].

3.1 Speaker Recognition Techniques

Two unsupervised generative probabilistic models were trained based on widely used state of the art speaker recognition techniques, namely: Gaussian Mixture Models-Universal Background Models (GMM-UBM) [31]; and iVectors-Gaussian Probabilistic Linear Discriminant Analysis (iVectors-GPDLA) [32].

The parametrization approaches followed are based on three well known families of parameters: Linear Predictive coefficients (LPC) [33], Mel-Frequency Cepstral Coefficients (MFCC) [34] and Relative Spectral-Perceptual Linear Prediction coefficients (RASTA-PLP) [35].

Seeking to maximize the performance of the system for the differential evaluation of the speech of PD patients with respect to controls, the different degrees of freedom of the aforementioned probabilistic models and of the parameterization approaches were analyzed using different metrics, mainly based on the accuracy and on the area under the receiving operating curve (AUC) [36], and using a k-folds crossvalidation strategy with 11 folds. The k-folds strategy was designed to ensure that all the data available belonging to the same speaker is either in the training or in the testing set, but never in both.

Regarding the parameterization front-end, we analyzed the influence of the window size (τ_{window}), the family of parameters (LPC, MFCC, RASTA-PLP), the number of static parameters extracted for each frame (i.e. the dimension of the feature space), the addition of the first and second derivatives (velocity and acceleration) [37] to the parameters extracted, and the time lag used for the kernel used to calculate the derivatives ($\tau_{derivative}$). With respect to the probabilistic models, the influence of the number of gaussians of the GMM-UBM, the iVector size, and the dimension of the vector of latent factor of the GLPDA was studied. More in depth details of the procedure followed can be found in [29].

The initial experiments were carried out modelling with GMM-UBM. Regarding the parameterization approach, the RASTA-PLP family of parameters complemented with the first and second derivatives provided the best results with both corpora using 12 coefficients. Results were quite similar when removing the RASTA filter in the parameterization front-end. The initial UBM model was trained using the *Albayzin* corpus, and the adaptation to obtain the final model was done following a Maximum a Posteriori (MAP) adaptation process of the means of the gaussians, thanks to the demonstrated ability of this method to work with small datasets.

With independence of the family of parameters, in all tests carried out using GMM-UBM, best results were obtained using Hamming windows with τ_{window} of 15 ms and $\tau_{derivative}$ of 40–45 ms. Using this probabilistic model, best discrimination was obtained with 4 components in the gaussian mixture (86 ± 7 of accuracy and AUC = 0.93).

Using the aforementioned configuration for the acoustic front-end, the modelling capabilities of the iVectors-GPLDA was also tested. The initial hypothesis is that this method should outperform the GMM-UBM but, although there were differences in the results obtained using the two probabilistic modelling approaches considered, differences were not very significant, due to the known limitations in the ability of the iVectors-GPLDA approach to work with small corpora, like those used. In any case, best results (87% ± 7 of accuracy and AUC = 0,94) were obtained using a iVectors-GPLDA model fed with eloquences of read text as acoustic material, with iVectors of dimension 50, and a size for the vector of latent factor of the GLPDA of 14. Using DDK utterances the accuracy decreased (82 ± 8 of accuracy and AUC = 0.90). More in depth details of the procedure followed and results can be found in [19]. Despite the iVectors-GPLDA improved the results with respect to those of the UBM-GMM, this approach showed a strong sensibility to its different degrees of freedom. Thus, in view of the small differences found, its simplicity, easiness of interpretation, and its robustness to the different degrees of freedom, the UBM-GMM approach was chosen for the remaining tests reported in this section.

For the sake of comparison, the results obtained are depicted in Fig. 1 using ROC Convex Hull Detection Error Tradeoff (ROCCH-DET) plots. The plot shows the results for the LPC, MFCC and RASTA-PLP parameterization approaches, all of them complemented with the velocity and acceleration of the static features, and with the optimum dimension of the feature space. Classification was carried out with GMM-UBM and iVectors-GPLDA. The best results are provided for one of the read sentences of the *GITA* corpus.

The acoustic task used to feed the system was also evaluated. Figure 2 illustrates the results obtained using sustained vowels, a DDK test, and two read sentences. The importance of the acoustic material is highlighted in the plot, suggesting that read sentences contain significant information, even more significant than the DDK test typically used in the clinic for the evaluation of the dysarthric speech. One interesting consequence is that results using read test are significantly better than with sustained vowels, but results with read test are dependent on the sentence (i.e. on the phonetic balance of the sentence).

This fact suggests the need for a careful design of the text to be read and a further in depth study of the influence of the individual phonemes and coarticulation effects. This aspect is studied later and some results are provided in this paper.

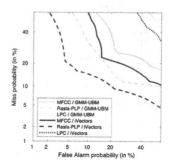

Fig. 1. ROCCH-DET curves for the LPC, MFCC and RASTA-PPLP parameterization approaches using a read sentence. The vectors of characteristics include the velocity and acceleration of the static features. Classification was carried out with GMM-UBM and iVectors-GPLDA.

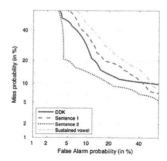

Fig. 2. ROCCH-DET curves for different acoustic materials. Worst results were obtained using sustained vowels.

Influence of the Derivatives. Following the hypothesis commented at the beginning of Sect. 3, and under the assumption that first and second derivatives (the kinetic coefficients, Δ and $\Delta\Delta$) of the static RASTA-PLP parameters characterize the speed and acceleration of changes in the vocal tract movements, their influence was also analyzed.

Figure 3 shows the mutual information of the individual RASTA-PLP static and kinetic coefficients belonging to the feature vector which leads to the best results using an iVectors-GPLDA model. The mutual information was calculated with respect to the classes represented (control/PD). In comparison with the mutual information obtained for the static RASTA-PLP coefficients, results report the relevance of the kinetic coefficients.

Classification tests were also carried out empirically removing the derivatives from the feature vector, using 12 RASTA-PLP static coefficients, a τ_{window} of 15 ms, and

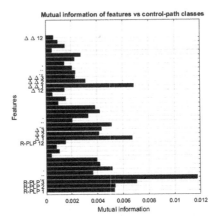

Fig. 3. Mutual information of the individual 12 RASTA-PLP (R-PLP in the plot) features and of their first and second derivatives (Δ and ΔΔ) with respect to the control/pathological classes.

GMM-UBM and iVectors-GPLDA classifiers. In the best scenario, results reported a maximum accuracy (71% ± 7 and AUC = 0.74), significantly below the one obtained including the derivatives, confirming the influence of the kinetic changes and the importance of the articulation. More in depth details of the procedure followed can be found in [19].

3.2   Envelope Analysis

Since the variations of the envelope of the speech are supposed to be indirectly linked with variations in both the mid-term air flow pressure and/or in the distribution of forces used to control the articulators, the envelope of the speech is supposed to be affected by both hypotheses. Since the DDK test is widely used in the clinic and the waveform is periodically repeated due to the characteristics of the test, we considered this speech task as a good benchmark test.

The method requires an initial estimation of the envelope of the speech recorded during the DDK test. It is automatically estimated interpolating with a spline over the local maxima and downsampling the results to 5 kHz. Once the envelope is calculated, its first and second derivatives were obtained using FIR anti-symmetric filters. Due to the smoothing effect introduced by the kernel, the selection of its length is a trade-off to avoid a noisy estimation and to precisely capture the most significant changes linked with the articulatory movements. The lengths of the kernels have been fixed empirically to maximize the Equal Error Rate (ERR) as a figure of merit separating controls and PD patients from a score. For this purpose, the variations of both sequences (i.e. speed and acceleration) were quantified using a permutation entropy (PE) [38] measurement using fixed-length speech frames of 1.37 s, overlapped 80%, and ensuring that each one contains at least 3 repetitions of the /pa/-/ta/-/ka/ sequence. PE was evaluated in an embedded domain, which requires the estimation of the time lag, τ, and the embedding dimension, D. τ was calculated for each frame using a criterion based on the estimation of the first minimum of the auto mutual information. Typical τ values are in the range $\{45, \dots, 100\}$ samples, with larger τ values for those patients with a lower rate of speech and vice-versa. The embedding dimension, D, is estimated based on the Cao's method [39]. A constant D = 6 value was estimated for the whole dataset, taking the maximum value of the individual embedding dimensions obtained for each of the speech frames.

The procedure led to a 50 ms long kernel for the speed se quence, and 40 ms for the acceleration. Figure 4 shows two examples representing the speech trace along with the envelope and its corresponding speed and acceleration for a control and a PD patient. The figure also depicts the 3D attractor in the embedded domain for both speakers.

In a second phase, each point of the attractor has been parameterized with 8 classic complexity measurements: Largest Lyapunov Exponent (LLE), Correlation Dimension (CD), Hurst Exponent (HE), Detrended Fluctuation Analysis (DFE), Recurrence Period Density Estimation (RPDE), Gaussian Kernel AE (GAE), Fuzzy Entropy (FE), and Permutation Entropy (PE). These entropy measurements were also extracted from the embedded domain with the parameters already identified.

Fusing the features extracted from the speed and from the acceleration, we obtained a feature vector with 16 components, which was used to feed a supervised discriminative system based on a support vector machine (SVM) with a linear kernel, which binary categorizes each frame of speech as control or PD.

A k-folds technique with 11 folds was used to estimate the overall performance of the system. Once the accuracy of the proposed scheme has been estimated, an algorithm based on Sequential Floating Feature Selection (SFFS) [40] was applied to reduce the dimensionality of the feature space, as well as to eliminate redundant information. The SFSS algorithm improved the performance of the system with only three features per sequence: CD, HE and PE features.

Figure 5 graphically illustrates the results obtained and in comparison with the baseline system considered based on speaker recognition techniques. The accuracy using the 14 complexity measures identified was 81.0 ± 7.6 (AUC = 0.87). Results improved after the SFFS feature selection procedure and reached 85.0 ± 6.9 (AUC = 0.91). More details can be found in [30].

4 Phonemic Analysis

The previous studies suggested not only the viability of an automatic evaluation of PD from the speech, but also the need of a further analysis of the individual acoustic units to evaluate the most significant ones, or those with a stronger correlation with the disease. The goal is not only to identify which are more significant to detect PD, but also to provide guidelines for the design of the protocols and speech tasks that might be more interesting for the analysis of PD due to their correlation with the disease (i.e. those units that are more affected by PD).

With the aforementioned in mind, we analyze in this section the effects introduced by PD in different units of speech, but following two approaches with a different degree of granularity. First, a study of the relevance of the individual phonemic units is carried out [25] and, second, a study is reported grouping the phonemes into different categories [41]: plosives, liquids, nasals, fricatives, and vowels.

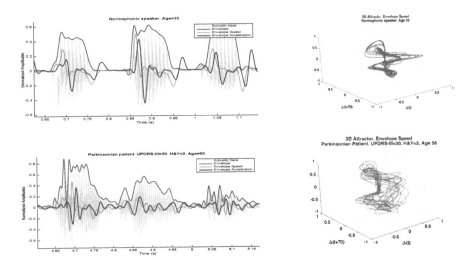

Fig. 4. Left: Speech trace with its envelope and an estimate of the velocity and acceleration of the envelope. Right: 3D attractors of the envelope of the speed sequence. Top: example corresponding to a young normophonic 35 yr old person. Down: example corresponding to a 56 yr old PD patient. The envelopes were calculated using 50 and 40 ms long smoothing kernels for the velocity and acceleration respectively. The speech traces correspond to one single utterance of the /pa/-/ta/-/ka/ test.

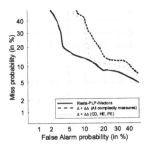

Fig. 5. ROCCH-DET plot of the baseline system based on speaker recognition techniques, for the system based on the kinetic analysis of the envelope using the complete feature set, and using a reduced number of features.

4.1 Phonetic Relevance

In our next study, we have developed a new classification scheme to establish independently relationships of the different phonemic units with the disease. The classification scheme used is a supervised probabilistic model based on a GMM-UBM, in which each component of the mixture is univocally liked with a different phonemic unit.

The process starts with an identification of the individual phonemic units. It was carried out following a speech forced alignment procedure, which is able to identify different phonemic units from a known written transcription of the eloquence. The forced alignment process provides labels for each phonemic unit and the time boundaries of each of them.

For the purpose of this work, a speaker independent Forced Alignment Model (FAM) was obtained by means of an iterative process based on a hybrid GMM-Hidden Markov Model (HMM) architecture, which was trained with the *FisherSP* auxiliary database using the Kaldi toolkit [42]. Once trained with the auxiliary corpus, and in view of the associated transcriptions, the FAM is able to automatically segment and label new utterances of a different corpus into their acoustic units. In general terms, the FAM trained identifies phonemic units, but does not distinguish among potential allophones that could be associated to a single phoneme. The phonemic units identified by the FAM are constrained by those established by default in the Kaldi toolkit. Thus, only plosive and fricative allophones of the phonemes /b/, /d/ and /g/ are considered, and the vowel /u/ is split in diphthong and hiatus, the last represented with the label /w/. Roughly speaking, the remaining phonemic units correspond to their orthographic counterparts. Such simplification is quite reasonable for the Spanish language thanks to its phonetic simplicity. For a complete list of the acoustic units used for this approach and their corresponding label in Kaldi, see the appendix in [25].

The FAM model is then used to identify the phonemic units of *Albayzin*, *GITA* and *Neurovoz* corpora. A set of 4800 sentences of the *Albayzin* corpus was parameterized using RASTA-PLP parameters along with their first and second derivatives, and the acoustic features obtained were then used to train an individual UBM in which the number of gaussians is equal to the number of phonemic units, so each of them is modelled by a single gaussian in a forced manner (i.e. each individual gaussian distribution of the model is forced to use the acoustic material available from a single phonemic unit). Once the UBM is obtained, and using all the sentences available, two separate GMM-UBMs (i.e. one for each class: control or PD) were trained by means of an adaptation procedure for both, the *GITA* and *Neurovoz,* corpora. The training of these two GMM-UBMs was carried out following a similar forced manner and parameterization procedure, but adapting the means of the UBM with a MAP procedure to each class (control or PD) of both corpora. More details can be found in [25].

Figure 6 illustrates graphically the modelling procedure followed, which we have called forced-UBM/forced-GMM. Each of the phonemes was modelled with a single gaussian density of the mixture, so the number of gaussians is equal to the number of acoustic units provided by the FAM method.

The process ends with two GMM-UBM models per corpus: one for each class (control and PD). Then, we can obtain a final score for each utterance subtracting the log-likelihood than a given sample belongs to the control from the log-likelihood of belonging to the PD group. These log-likelihoods were individually calculated averaging the likelihood in the log-domain obtained for each frame. The final score is compared with a threshold at the Equal Error Rate (EER) point (the point in which false acceptance rate equals false rejection rate) to identify the class membership.

Therefore, the final score is calculated for each utterance. But taking advantage of the phonemic labelling of the utterances and the unambiguous correspondence among the acoustic units and each of the gaussian components of the GMM, we can also compute a score for each individual phoneme.

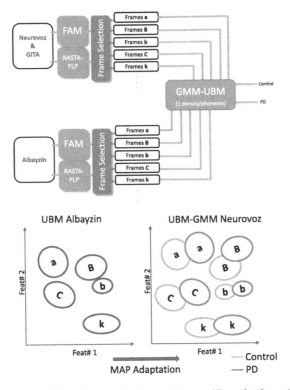

Fig. 6. Forced-UBM/forced-GMM general scheme. The auxiliary database (*Albayzin*) and the adaptation corpus (*Neurovoz* and/or *GITA*) were modelled with a gaussian mixture in which each gaussian distribution is adjusted using the acoustic material available from a single phonemic unit.

Taking advantage of the possibility to obtain a score for each phoneme, the automatic detection of PD was improved by fusing the scores obtained for each unit with a logistic regression. To this respect, the accuracy obtained for each phoneme after the adaptation process of the forced-UBM/forced-GMM classifier is used to create a weight vector that is used in the ulterior computation of the class membership. This weight vector increases the significance of the most relevant phonemes during the fusion stage. Thus, if a phonemic unit demonstrates better discrimination capabilities than others in the training subset, the weighting vector makes the frames of that phonemic unit more relevant in the final computation of the score for a new test utterance.

A k-folds crossvalidation procedure with 11 folds was followed to evaluate the methods. Figure 7 shows the results obtained for a binary decision between controls and PD patients for each phonemic unit and for both corpora: *GITA* and *Neurovoz*. The plot depicts the average sensitivity and specificity obtained for each phonemic unit, having been calculated for each frame of speech analyzed. Although there are differences among both corpora due to dialectal divergences and due to the acoustic context of each unit (i.e. the position of the different phonemic units in the sentences are different in each corpus), a rough conclusion is that the most significant units are /C/, /

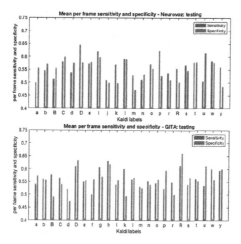

Fig. 7. Mean per frame sensitivity and specificity using the *Neurovoz* (top) and *GITA* (down) corpora. The horizontal line at 0.5 would represent a random decision.

D/, /g/ and /R/ (those with higher narrowing but without burst); and the less influential are /m/ and /B/.

Regarding the overall accuracy of the system detecting the class that an utterance belongs to (control of PD), obtained fusing the individual scores given by each phonemic unit, results are similar for the *GITA* (78.0 ± 8 with AUC = 0.88) and *Neurovoz* (81.0 ± 9 with AUC = 0.87) corpora. These results are illustrated graphically in Fig. 9 using ROCCH-DET plots, and in Fig. 8 showing the AUC for the different speech tasks recorded in both corpora, namely: monologue, DDK test, and fixed text (Text Dependent Utterances-TDU).

Figure 8 also shows the results in a cross-corpora domain (models trained with one corpus and tested with the other). As expected, the accuracy in this last scenario significantly decreased, but the system still keeps its discrimination capabilities, suggesting the potentiality of the techniques described.

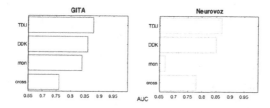

Fig. 8. AUC obtained for the *Neurovoz* (right) and *GITA* (left) corpora for different speech tasks. The legends correspond to the speech task: "TDU" corresponds to fixed text, "DDK" to the DDK test, "mon" to a monologue, and "cross" to a cross-corpora experiment.

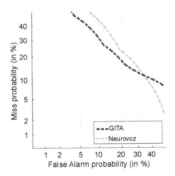

Fig. 9. ROCCH-DET plot that shows the behavior of the automatic detection system for both corpora: *Neurovoz* and *GITA*.

4.2   Phonemic Grouping

Our next study is complementary to the one presented in the previous section. At this stage, we developed a new classification scheme to evaluate the relationship of different phonemic groups with the disease. As in the previous section, the classification scheme is based on a supervised probabilistic model, but it was developed for each phonemic group identified for the Spanish language, instead of for each individual phoneme. The process uses the accuracy of the automatic detection system as a figure of merit, but the main goal is to evaluate the influence of the manner of articulation in the speech of parkinsonian people through identification of those segments that are more relevant for the automatic system.

The acoustic segments were selected according to the manner of articulation following a procedure that we have called *phonemic grouping*. The study uses one of the categorizations established in [43] for the allophones present in the Spanish language. Broadly speaking, the complete set of allophones is divided into five categories according to the type of articulatory movements and the degree of narrowing of the vocal tract, namely: plosives, fricatives, affricates, liquids, and nasals. These five classes are considered the manner classes of the Spanish language, but are complemented in this approach with an additional sixth class corresponding to the vowels.

Like in the previous method (Sect. 4.1), the process starts with a forced alignment of the training corpus *Albayzin* using the same FAM method. The FAM divides the speech into its corresponding phonemes, also providing their time boundaries, so these boundaries were used to identify the starting and ending point of each phonemic unit. See [25] for a complete list of the acoustic units used.

The speech is later parameterized with the same acoustic front end used in the former methods, consisting of 12 RASTA-PLP coefficients complemented with their first and second derivatives, and extracted from 15 ms Hamming windows. Using the time boundaries given by the FAM method, the vectors of parameters are then clustered according to the category they belong to, and the acoustic material of each of the six clusters identified was used to train a probabilistic model, leading to five different UBMs, one for each category. All the available utterances in the corpus were pooled to train the background models. For the sake of simplicity, affricates are left aside since they are underrepresented in the corpora used (they represent less than 3% in the Spanish language).

Once the UBMs were trained, for each of the aforementioned categories and for each of the corpora available, we developed a GMM-UBM model for each class (one for control speakers and another for the PD patients). For this purpose a MAP adaptation was carried out for every UBM obtained from *Albayzin* to obtain new GMM-UBM models for the *GITA* and *Neurovoz* corpora. Only means of the components are adapted. To this respect, one possibility was to segment the adaptation corpora using the FAM model already developed and later adapt each of the UBMs to each category using the specific data of each category in the adaptation corpora; or to adapt the different UBMs corresponding to each category using all the acoustic information available. The second was preferred since it provided higher accuracies. Figure 10 illustrates graphically the method used for the phonemic grouping.

For each of the GMM-UBM models corresponding to each category, and for every utterance, two probability estimates were obtained calculating the log-likelihood of each feature vector belonging to the control or PD class, and averaging the results with the number of frames extracted. Formerly, for each utterance and for each phonemic group, a final score is obtained calculating the subtracting the averaged log-likelihoods. The decision about class membership is taken comparing the final score with a threshold established at the EER point. Since the process involves five GMM-UBM models (one per category) the process ends with five different scores, which let us evaluate the individual discrimination capabilities of each phonemic group.

Additionally, a new mark was calculated fusing the scores obtained from the different GMM-UBM models developed for each of the five possible categories –or phonemic groups–. They were fused following all the possible combinations of n − tuples, from n = 2 to 5, providing a new score calculated by logistic regression. Therefore, for a given speaker and speech task, a new set of marks were calculated, each score coming from a different combination of groups of phonemes. This approach let us improve the results of accuracy, but also to evaluate the complementarity of the different groups for the differential evaluation of PD. The fusing procedure was carried out using the same number of RASTA-PLP parameters and the same number of gaussians in the probabilistic models.

Like in the former scenarios, the evaluation was carried out following a k-folds cross validation procedure with 11 folds, and experiments were carried out using the different speech tasks available in the adaptation corpora: text dependent utterances, the DDK test, and monologues.

Figure 11 shows graphically the discrimination results in terms of AUC for the different categories, speech tasks and adaptation corpora used. Plosives provided the best accuracy (85.0 ± 7 with AUC = 0.91) in the *GITA* corpus; and fricatives (89.0 ± 7 with AUC = 0.93) in *Neurovoz*. The same behavior appeared using text-dependent utterances and the recorded monologues. Results are detailed numerically in Table 2.

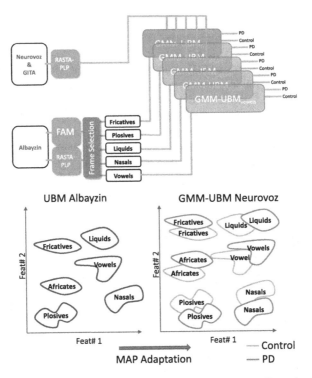

Fig. 10. General scheme of the phonemic grouping process. The auxiliary database (*Albayzin*) and the adaptation corpus (*Neurovoz* and/or *GITA*) were modelled with a gaussian mixture in which each gaussian distribution for each class (control or PD) is adjusted using the acoustic material available from a single phonemic group.

Figure 11 also shows graphically the results in the cross-corpora experiments, which are detailed in Table 3. Table 3 shows an interesting result: as expected due to the dialectal divergences and to the different acoustic material, cross-corpora experiments significantly decreased the accuracy for all categories, except for vowels (in comparison with the results found in Sect. 3.1). This is attributed to the fact that the dialectal divergences between Colombian and European Spanish primary affect the remaining acoustic units but keeping the same vowels.

In addition, Table 4 presents the results fusing the scores for both adaptation corpora. For *Neurovoz*, combined models of fricatives and vowels yielded the best results (89.0 ± 7 with AUC = 0.95), whereas in *GITA* best results appeared for models combining plosives and liquids (84.0 ± 7 with AUC = 0.90), meaning that the fusion process is able to improve the performance of the system to automatically detect PD. More complex fusion schemes have not reported better discrimination capabilities.

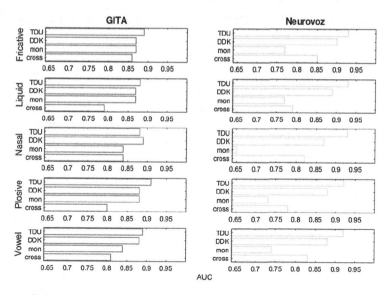

Fig. 11. AUC for the experiments carried out with *GITA* (left) and *Neurovoz* (right) corpora. Results are referred to the three proposed tasks recorded in both corpora, namely: monologue (represented as "mon"), DDK test (represented as "DDK"), and text dependent utterances (represented as "TDU"). Also results with cross-corpora trials are provided (represented as "cross").

Table 2. Results for the three approaches employing *GITA* and *Neurovoz* adapting the UBM created with *Albayzin*.

Speech task	Phonemic group	GITA				Neurovoz			
		Accu.	AUC	Sens.	Spec.	Accu.	AUC	Sens.	Spec.
TDU	Fricatives	82 ± 8	0.89	0.82	0.82	**89 ± 7**	**0.93**	**0.87**	**0.91**
	Liquids	81 ± 8	0.88	0.74	0.88	87 ± 7	0.93	0.87	0.88
	Nasals	82 ± 8	0.88	0.82	0.82	85 ± 8	0.93	0.85	0.84
	Plosives	**85 ± 7**	**0.91**	**0.82**	**0.88**	86 ± 8	0.92	0.85	0.88
	Vowels	82 ± 8	0.89	0.76	0.88	85 ± 8	0.92	0.83	0.88
DDK	Fricatives	80 ± 8	0.87	0.8	0.8	83 ± 9	0.9	0.89	0.73
	Liquids	82 ± 8	0.87	0.8	0.84	81 ± 9	0.89	0.85	0.73
	Nasals	83 ± 7	0.89	0.86	0.8	82 ± 9	0.87	0.85	0.77
	Plosives	82 ± 8	0.88	0.86	0.78	86 ± 8	0.88	0.89	0.81
	Vowels	83 ± 7	0.88	0.86	0.8	81 ± 9	0.88	0.87	0.69
Monol	Fricatives	80 ± 8	0.87	0.71	0.88	74 ± 12	0.77	0.47	0.9
	Liquids	80 ± 8	0.87	0.73	0.86	66 ± 14	0.77	0.06	1
	Nasals	77 ± 8	0.84	0.69	0.84	70 ± 13	0.65	0.41	0.87
	Plosives	80 ± 8	0.88	0.71	0.88	70 ± 13	0.73	0.41	0.87
	Vowels	78 ± 8	0.84	0.76	0.8	72 ± 13	0.74	0.65	0.77

Table 3. Cross-corpora results in *GITA* and *Neurovoz* corpora employing *Albayzin* for the UBM.

	GITA				Neurovoz			
	Accuracy	AUC	Sens	Spec.	Accuracy	AUC	Sens	Spec.
Fricatives	74 ± 9	0.86	0.66	0.82	75 ± 10	0.85	0.76	0.73
Liquids	69 ± 9	0.79	0.94	0.44	74 ± 10	0.79	0.87	0.5
Nasals	75 ± 8	0.84	0.86	0.64	74 ± 10	0.82	0.78	0.65
Plosives	74 ± 9	0.8	0.86	0.62	72 ± 10	0.78	0.93	0.35
Vowels	72 ± 9	0.81	0.7	0.74	81 ± 9	0.83	0.91	0.62

Table 4. Results after fusing the scores for both corpora: *GITA* and Neurovoz.

	GITA			Neurovoz		
		Accuracy	AUC		Accuracy	AUC
TDU	Plosive-liquid	**84 ± 7**	0.9	Fricative-vowel	**89 ± 7**	**0.95**
DDK	Nasal-liquid	83 ± 7	0.88	Liquid-vowel	83 ± 9	0.89
Monologue	Liquid-vowel	82 ± 8	0.89	Plosive-nasal-vowel	77 ± 12	0.79

5   Conclusions and Discussion

The objective of this study is twofold: first, an evaluation of different methods based on speaker recognition techniques for the automatic detection of PD, looking for the one with better discrimination capabilities; and second, to automatically extract relevant knowledge about the characteristics and units of the speech that are more affected by the disease.

Regarding the first goal, this chapter compares the results obtained using different approaches for the automatic detection of PD from the speech. Having in mind the confidence intervals and the small differences in accuracy and AUC found among most of the experimental approaches developed, we can conclude that the dissimilarities are not strong enough to completely ensure that those systems, methods or setups that provided better accuracies are the best approaches for our purpose. Nevertheless, the parallelisms found with the two corpora used, in the cross-corpora experiments, the consistency in the results found among the different approaches followed, along with the higher accuracy values obtained for some of them, provide significant evidences of the advantages of some methods and setups with respect to others. In view of it, the results obtained using the phonemic grouping approach (Sect. 4.2) are considered the most relevant of those developed. The methods based on the classic speaker recognition techniques (Sect. 3.1) and on the analysis of the envelope (Sect. 3.2) also revealed a very good accuracy, followed by the methods developed for the identification of the most significant phonemic units (Sect. 4.1).

Regarding the parameterization approaches used, results with LPC are significantly worse than with MFCC, PLP and RASTA-PLP, so the first approach was discarded, even when it is supposed to model well the information of the vocal tract. The differences among MFCC and RASTA-PLP were not very significant, but the second is preferred, due to the better accuracy reported and its potential to better model changes in the vocal tract.

With respect to the probabilistic classification approaches used, the GMM-UBM methods typically provided the best results. Despite of its simplicity, the GMM-UBM approach is able to deal well with small datasets, which supports why the results outperformed the approach based on iVectors-GPLDA. Although the iVectors-GPLDA methodology usually improves the results in speaker recognition tasks, the advantages of this technique only emerge with large corpora and a big amount of classes to be identified. Its simplicity also let us define models with a clear physical interpretation, which is relevant for our second goal. GMM-UBM also demonstrated to be less sensitive to the setup and requires less computational cost.

Regarding the second goal, linked with the potential of the proposed methods to extract relevant knowledge from the parkinsonian speech, results suggest that the kinetic information that might be extracted from the speech provides relevant information to improve the results and the modelling capabilities. To this respect two different methods (Sect. 3.1 and Sect. 3.2) were developed introducing this type of information, leading to similar results. Both approaches reveal the importance of the kinetic analysis in the design of automatic systems for the differential evaluation of PD. The relevance of the kinetic information is consistent with the idea that PD patients have more difficulties –among others- in restoring a more rapid selection of the cues for the next stage of the motor activation, leading to a tendency to make the stops, gaps and voice onset times shorter, to increase the vowel onset and offset times, and to decrease the amplitudes of the stable parts of the vowels. In other words, the movements of the speech articulators are clearly affected in their extent, speed and acceleration, being one of the major signs of the dysarthria developed by parkinsonian patients [44–46]. It means that the velocity and the acceleration of the movements of the vocal tract are significantly altered with respect to control patients. Thus, including these measurements extracted from time varying features characterizing aspects that might be related to the vocal tract movements is considered relevant for our purpose.

It is worth to note that, despite of the differences in the two methods used for both kinetic approaches developed, both kernels used to estimate the derivatives are empirically fixed around 40–50 ms long, which represents around half of the median duration of a phoneme, which is usually around 90 ms [47]. This finding is considered significant to avoid introducing oversmoothing effects that could merge together information from different phonemes.

Regarding the phonemic analysis, the proposed techniques have been able to automatically identify and compare which allophones of the speech are more affected by PD, revealing that phonation and/or articulation of every single allophone are affected by PD to a certain degree, and identifying which allophones are the most significant (Sect. 4.1). On the other hand, the phonemic grouping techniques (Sect. 4.2) developed reveals that plosives and fricatives are widely affected by PD. This is explained by the spirantization effect introduced by the disease. But results also show that the remaining groups identified (i.e. liquids, nasals, and vowels) contain significant information to characterize the disease. In contrast with what was known in the literature, that mainly put the focus on the analysis of obstruents, the study suggests that all manner classes are significantly affected by PD to a certain degree.

Individually, the phonemic study carried out also (Sect. 4.1) also suggests that those units that require a higher narrowing of the vocal tract (/C/, /d/, /g/ and /R/) are more affected by the disease, which is in consonance with the aforementioned results obtained for the phonemic grouping (Sect. 4.2) using different techniques. On the other hand, others such as /B/ and /w/ are less influential, which is in consonance with the studies in [2, 48].

In any case, results report differences in both corpora used, not only in terms of accuracy, but also in terms of phonemic relevance. These differences are attributable to the dialectal dissimilarities between the European and Colombian Spanish, but also due to the differences in the acoustic material used, since the read sentences are different in both corpora leading to different coarticulation effects for each phonemic unit extracted. Note that, due to the small size of the corpora, the phonemic models (with or without grouping) are constrained by the side effects of the adjacent units.

Results suggest an upper limit around 90% of accuracy in the approaches developed, which might be due to the techniques used or to the data used, but also to other considerations that are important to be taken into account: statistics show that approximately 70–90% of the patients with PD develop dysarthria during the course of the disease [12, 13]. On the other hand, literature also reports that using current diagnosis techniques, 2–4% of the patients might be misdiagnosed [49]. Additionally, it is known a decline in the planning and execution of speech production in healthy older adults [50]. Inevitably, these statistics reveal that there must be errors in the labelling of the population of the different corpora used, also meaning that there is a potential "glass ceiling" in the expected accuracy which might be close to the aforementioned 90%. Thus, accuracies of 100% might probably be unrealistic, so the future efforts should be directed to extract knowledge from the speech rather than to improve the classification accuracy.

Despite the interest of the results provided, it is also worth to note their limitations, which are mainly grounded on the number of patients recorded in both corpora and on the limited amount of acoustic material used. The techniques developed are promising not only for the automatic detection of PD, but also to automatically extract relevant knowledge about the characteristics and units of the speech that are more affected by the disease. However, an in depth demonstration of the usefulness of these techniques and the possibility to extrapolate to other languages, requires a validation with much larger corpora. In any case, the conclusions obtained –mainly those related with the phonemic grouping– are of interest to guide the definition of new protocols to record new corpora, and to establish some common grounds in the automatic analysis of parkinsonian speech.

Acknowledgements. This work was supported by the Spanish Ministry of Economy and Competitiveness under grant DPI2017-83405-R1 and with a MIT-Spain Global Seed Funds Award. Special thanks to R. Orozco-Arroyave, J. D. Arias-Londoño, and J. F. Vargas-Bonilla of the Universidad de Antioquia for sharing the *GITA* corpus of speakers.

References

1. Djuric-Jovicic, M.D., Jovicic, N.S., Radovanovic, S.M., Stankovic, I.D., Popovic, M.B., Kostic, V.S.: Automatic identification and classification of freezing of gait episodes in parkinson's disease patients. IEEE Trans. Neural Syst. Rehabil. Eng. **22**(3), 685–694 (2014)
2. Rusz, J., Cmejla, R., Tykalova, T., Ruzickova, H., Klempir, J., Majerova, V., et al.: Imprecise vowel articulation as a potential early marker of Parkinson's disease: effect of speaking task. J. Acoust. Soc. Am. **134**(3), 2171–2181 (2013)
3. Kraus, P.H., Lemke, M.R., Reichmann, H.: Kinetic tremor in Parkinson's disease – an underrated symptom. J. Neural Trans. **113**(7), 845–853 (2006)
4. Mitsi, G., Mendoza, E.U., Wissel, B.D., Barbopoulou, E., Dwivedi, A.K., Tsoulos, I., et al.: Biometric digital health technology for measuring motor function in Parkinson's disease: results from a feasibility and patient satisfaction study. Front. Neurol. **8**, 273 (2017)
5. Adams, W.R.: High-accuracy detection of early Parkinson's Disease using multiple characteristics of finger movement while typing. PLoS One **12**(11), e0188226 (2017). Fröhlich H, editor
6. Skodda, S., Grönheit, W., Mancinelli, N., Schlegel, U.: Progression of voice and speech impairment in the course of Parkinson's disease: a longitudinal study. Parkinsons Dis. (2013)
7. Hughes, A.J., Daniel, S.E., Lees, A.J.: Improved accuracy of clinical diagnosis of Lewy body Parkinson's disease. Neurology **57**(8), 1497–1499 (2001)
8. Darley, F.L., Aronson, A.E., Brown, J.R.: Differential diagnostic patterns of dysarthria. J. Speech Lang. Hear Res. **12**(2), 246 (1969)
9. Darley, F.L., Aronson, A.E., Brown, J.R.: Clusters of deviant speech dimensions in the dysarthrias. J. Speech Lang. Hear Res. **12**(3), 462 (1969)
10. Duffy, J.R.: Motor Speech Disorders. Substrates, Differential Diagnosis and Management, 2nd ed. Elsevier, St. Louis (2005)
11. Pinto, S., Ozsancak, C., Tripoliti, E., Thobois, S., Limousin-Dowsey, P., Auzou, P.: Treatments for dysarthria in Parkinson's disease. Neurology **3**, 547–556 (2004)
12. Ramig, L.O., Fox, C., Sapir, S.: Speech treatment for Parkinson's disease. Expert Rev. Neurother. **8**, 297–309 (2008)
13. Logemann, J.A., Fisher, H.B., Boshes, B., Blonsky, E.R.: Frequency and cooccurrence of vocal tract dysfunctions in the speech of a large sample of Parkinson patients. J. Speech Hear. Disord. **43**(1), 47–57 (1978)
14. Tjaden, K.: Speech and swallowing in Parkinson's disease. Top. Geriatr. Rehabil. **24**, 115–126 (2008)
15. Thanvi, B., Lo, N., Robinson, T.: Levodopa-induced dyskinesia in Parkinson's disease: clinical features, pathogenesis, prevention and treatment. Postgrad. Med. J. **8**, 384–388 (2007)
16. Tanaka, Y., Nishio, M., Niimi, S.: Vocal acoustic characteristics of patients with Parkinson's disease. Folia Phoniatr. Logop. **63**(5), 223–230 (2011)
17. Kent, T.R.D., Vorperian, H.K., Kent, J.F., Duffy, J.R.: Voice dysfunction in dysarthria: application of the multi-dimensional voice program. J. Commun. Disord. **36**, 281–306 (2003)
18. Midi, I., Dogan, M., Koseoglu, M., Can, G., Sehitoglu, M.A., Gunal, D.I.: Voice abnormalities and their relation with motor dysfunction in Parkinson's disease. Acta Neurol. Scand. **117**, 26–34 (2007)
19. Moro-Velázquez, L., Gómez-García, J.A., Godino-Llorente, J.I., Villalba, J., Orozco-Arroyave, J.R., Dehak, N.: Analysis of speaker recognition methodologies and the influence of kinetic changes to automatically detect Parkinson's Disease. Appl. Soft Comput. **62**, 649–666 (2018)

20. Tsanas, A., Little, M.A., McSharry, P.E., Spielman, J., Ramig, L.O.: Novel speech signal processing algorithms for high-accuracy classification of Parkinsons disease. IEEE Trans. Biomed. Eng. **59**(5), 1264–1271 (2012)

21. Tsanas, A., Little, M.: Accurate telemonitoring of Parkinson's disease progression by noninvasive speech tests. IEEE Trans. Biomed. Eng. **57**(4), 884–893 (2010)

22. Ackermann, H., Hertrich, I., Hehr, T.: Oral diadochokinesis in neurological dysarthrias. Folia Phoniatr. Logop. **47**(1), 15–23 (1995)

23. Chenausky, K., MacAuslan, J., Goldhor, R.: Acoustic analysis of PD speech. Parkinsons Dis. (2011)

24. Asgari, M., Shafran, I.: Predicting severity of Parkinson's disease from speech. Annu. Int. Conf. IEEE Eng. Med. Biol. Soc. **2010**, 5201–5204 (2010). https://doi.org/10.1109/IEMBS. 2010.5626104

25. Moro-Velazquez, L., Gomez-Garcia, J.A., Godino-Llorente, J.I., Villalba, J., Rusz, J., Shattuck-Hufnagel, S., et al.: A forced gaussians based methodology for the differential evaluation of Parkinson's Disease by means of speech processing. Biomed. Signal Process. Control. **48**, 205–220 (2019)

26. Orozco, J.R., Arias, J.D., Vargas, J.F., González Rátiva, M.C., Nöth, E.: New Spanish speech corpus database for the analysis of people suffering from Parkinson's disease. In: Lr 2014 Proceedings of Ninth International Conference on Language Resource Evaluation, pp. 342–347 (2014)

27. Moreno, A., et al.: Albayzín speech database: Design of the phonetic corpus. In: Proceedings of EUROSPEECH, 175–178 (1993)

28. Graff, D., Huang, S., Cartagena, I., Kevin Walker, C.C.: Fisher Spanish Speech. Linguistic Data Consortium, Philadelphia (2010)

29. Moro-Velázquez, L., Gómez-García, J.A., Godino-Llorente, J.I., Villalba, J., Orozco-Arroyave, J.R., Dehak, N.: Analysis of speaker recognition methodologies and the influence of kinetic changes to automatically detect Parkinson's Disease. Appl. Soft Comput. J. **1**(62), 649–666 (2018)

30. Godino-Llorente, J.I., Shattuck-Hufnagel, S., Choi, J.Y., Moro-Velázquez, L., Gómez-García, J.A.: Towards the identification of Idiopathic Parkinson's Disease from the speech. new articulatory kinetic biomarkers. PLoS One **12**(12), e0189583 (2017). Jäncke L, editor

31. Reynolds, D.A., Quatieri, T.F., Dunn, R.B.: Speaker verification using adapted Gaussian mixture models. Digit Signal Process. **10**, 19–41 (2000)

32. Garcia-Romero, D., Espy-Wilson, C.Y.: Analysis of I-vector Length normalization in speaker recognition systems. In: Interspeech, Florence, Italy, pp. 249–252 (2011)

33. Shaughnessy, D.O.: Linear predictive coding. IEEE Potentials **7**(1), 29–32 (1988)

34. Davis, S., Mermelstein, P.: Comparison of parametric representations for monosyllabic word recognition in continuously spoken sentences. IEEE Trans. Acoust. **28**(4), 357–366 (1980)

35. Hermansky, H., Morgan, N.: RASTA processing of speech. IEEE Trans. Speech Audio Process. **2**(4), 578–589 (1994)

36. Fawcett, T.: An introduction to ROC analysis. Pattern Recognit. Lett. **27**(8), 861–874 (2006)

37. Furui, S.: Speaker-independent isolated word recognition using dynamic features of speech spectrum. IEEE Trans. Acoust. **34**(1), 52–59 (1986)

38. Zanin, M., Zunino, L., Rosso, O.A., Papo, D.: Permutation entropy and its main biomedical and econophysics applications: a review. Entroppy **14**, 1553–1577 (2012)

39. Cao, L.: Practical method for determining the minimum embedding dimension of a scalar time series. Phys. D **110**(1–2), 43–50 (1997)

40. Pudil, P., Novovičová, J., Kittler, J.: Floating search methods in feature selection. Pattern Recognit. Lett. **15**(11), 1119–1125 (1994)

41. Moro-Velazquez, L., Gomez-Garcia, J.A., Godino-Llorente, J.I., Grandas-Perez, F., Shattuck-Hufnagel, S., Yagüe-Jimenez, V., et al.: Phonetic relevance and phonemic grouping of speech in the automatic detection of Parkinson's Disease. Sci. Rep. **9**(1), 1–16 (2019)

42. Povey, D., Ghoshal, A., Boulianne, G., Burget, L., Glembek, O., Goel, N., et al.: The Kaldi speech recognition toolkit. In: IEEE 2011 Workshop on Automatic Speech Recognition and Understanding, Big Island, Hawaii, US (2011)

43. Quilis-Morales, A.: Tratado de fonología y fonética españolas. 2nd ed. Gredos, Madrid (1993)

44. Walsh, A.S.B.: Basic parameters of articulatory movements and acoustics in individuals with Parkinson's Disease. Mov. Disord. **27**(7), 843–850 (2012)

45. Wong, M.N., Murdoch, B.E., Whelan, B.M.: Kinematic analysis of lingual function in dysarthric speakers with Parkinson's disease: an electromagnetic articulograph study. Int. J. Speech Lang. Pathol. **12**(5), 414–425 (2010)

46. Aekermann, H., Gröne, B.F., Hoch, G., Schönle, P.W.: Speech freezing in parkinson's disease: a kinematic analysis of orofacial movements by means of electromagnetic articulography. Folia Phoniatr. Logop. **45**(2), 84–89 (1993)

47. Stevens, K.: Acoustc Phonetics. MIT Press, Cambridge (2000)

48. Tjaden, K., Lam, J., Wilding, G.: Vowel acoustics in Parkinson's disease and multiple sclerosis: comparison of clear, loud, and slow speaking conditions. J. Speech Lang. Hear. Res. **56**(5), 1485–1502 (2013)

49. Hughes. A., Daniel. S., Kilford. L.: Accuracy of clinical diagnosis of idiopathic Parkinson's disease: a clinico-pathological study of 100 cases. J. Neurol. (1992)

50. Tremblay, P., Deschamps, I., Bédard, P., Tessier, M.H., Carrier, M., Thibeault, M.: Aging of speech production, from articulatory accuracy to motor timing. Psychol. Aging **33**(7), 1022–1034 (2018)

Predicting UPDRS Scores in Parkinson's Disease Using Voice Signals: A Deep Learning/Transfer-Learning-Based Approach

Julián D. Arias-Londoño[1]([⊠]) [ID] and Jorge A. Gómez-García[2] [ID]

[1] Department of Systems Engineering, Universidad de Antioquia,
Calle 67 No. 53 - 108, 050010 Medellín, Colombia
julian.ariasl@udea.edu.co
[2] Bioengineering and Optoelectronics Lab, Universidad Politécnica de Madrid,
Ctra. Valencia, km. 7, 28031 Madrid, Spain
jorge.gomez.garcia@upm.es

Abstract. In the last years, literature exhibits successful results in the automatic detection of Parkinson's disease using voice/speech, especially for patients in medium or late stages of the disorder. By contrast, the prediction of the UPDRS scores -used to assess the severity of the disorder or the efficacy of treatments- has been shown to perform mostly poor. These results could be explained by the need of more complex machine learning models compared to the detection case, and the lack of large databases for properly training artificial intelligence models. To analyse possible solutions to these problems, this work will explore the potentiality of *Deep Neural Network* (DNN) and *Convolutional Neural Network* (CNN) models, along transfer learning approaches, for the automatic prediction of the UPDRS scores. Experiments are carried out using feature engineering and feature learning methodologies. In particular for feature engineering, a series of well-know features that are used to characterise vocal conditions are employed to train a DNN. Likewise, the feature learning approach is based on transformation of the input speech using Modulation spectra transformations to train a CNN, considering a transfer learning approach. For transfer learning, the networks will be trained using voice signals from patients of databases of organic and functional voice pathologies; following a network architecture that has been proven successful recently for voice quality assessment using the GRB scale. The approach includes the combination of feature learning and feature engineering approaches using a multimodal strategy. The fine-tuning procedure of the last layers in the second network will be carried out using two databases of PD patients. The results present insights about the potential of deep learning along with transfer learning strategies for the prediction of UPDRS score in parkinsonian speechs.

Keywords: Parkinson's disease detection/assessment · Voice signals · Deep learning · Transfer learning

© Springer Nature Switzerland AG 2020
J. I. Godino-Llorente (Ed.): AAPS 2019, CCIS 1295, pp. 100–123, 2020.
https://doi.org/10.1007/978-3-030-65654-6_6

1   Introduction

Parkinson's disease (PD) is a neurodegenerative disorder that affects the centers of dopamine production in the basal ganglia. It is the second most common neurodegenerative disorder after Alzheimer's disease, with a prevalence of about 0–3% of the population in industrialised countries [13]. Just in Europe in 2010, the cost of the disorder was estimated in about €14 billion. However, as a result of the aging trend of the population it is expected that the number of patients with PD will double by 2030 [20], and subsequently, the costs to the health systems will likely increase.

The typical diagnosis and assessment procedures of PD involve a series of clinical examinations based on the analysis of cardinal motor cues such as bradykinesia, rigidity, postural instability and resting tremor; supported by other non-motor cues like depression, eating and salivation problems, etc. [37]. The result of these procedures is a diagnosis about the state of the patient. To complement the evaluation of PD, a clinical assessment is often carried out to quantify the severity of the pathology by means of the application of clinical rating scales. Among the existing scales, one of the most popular is the *Unified Parkinson's Disease Rating Scale* (UPDRS) [8]. This is composed of 42 items, each item ranging from 0 (normal) to 4 (severe), summing up a total score of 199, and which are divided into 4 sections according to the characteristics they measure [8]: (i) mentation, behaviour, and mood (0–16 points); (ii) activities of daily living (0–52 points); (iii) motor examination (0–108 points); (iv) complications of therapy (0–23 points). A newer version of the scale was proposed by the Movement Disorder Society [15], conceived to be more complete, homogeneous, and with better clinimetric properties than the UPDRS scale. This new scale is called MDS-UPDRS, and like the UPDRS scale, is composed of 4 sections that slightly differ from its predecessor. The MDS-UPDRS include 65 items summing up a maximum of 260, which are as follow: (i) non-motor experiences of daily living (0–52 points); (ii) motor experiences of daily living (0–52 points); (iii) motor examination (0–132 points); (iv) motor complications (0–24 points).

Several troubles arise in the analysis of the cardinal signs of the disorder to diagnose and assess PD. In one hand, a disadvantage on the use of the assessment scales is the subjectivity of the process, since these procedures require the evaluation of several items by the clinical expert and, in the case of the MDS-UPDRS, self-assessments made by the patient. For these reasons, factors such as the experience of the evaluator, the cognitive status, mood of the patient, etc., might compromise the reliability of the evaluation. On the other hand, and despite the increasing knowledge about PD, the neuropathological diagnosis during autopsy is still the gold standard to confirm the presence of the disorder. Studies comparing the performance of the analysis of the cardinal clinical signs versus neuropathological diagnosis, attained correct rates in about 90% of the cases [23]. Because of that, a lot of effort is being carried out to increase the reliability of the diagnosis, decrease the time taken to make a diagnosis, and make the assessment of the pathology more objective. Indeed, numerous investigations are been dedicated to the study of new objective biomarkers that might support and enhance the current clinical procedures, assisted by engineering tools such as those provided by signal processing and artificial intelligence methodologies. In particular, a growing body of research has been carried out using non-invasive biomarkers including those derived from medical imaging [43], audio-visual analysis of motor cues [34], speech [31], etc. With respect to speech, encouraging results have been obtained for PD diagnosis -and more modestly for assessment- [31,42], mainly because speech production requires very precise and complex movements that are affected by PD, resulting in dysphonia, dysarthria and disprosody. These phenomena have been successfully characterised and employed for the design of automatic systems -with diverging degrees of success depending on the dataset and experimental conditions considered-.

Traditionally, the analysis of parkinsonian speech has been addressed using methodologies that have been primarily developed for the assessment of speech pathologies (organic, functional, multiple etiologies), although, in the last few years, new features or pipelines specifically designed to capture relevant characteristics of the parkinsonian speech have arisen [30]. There have been as well, some timid efforts to translate some of the methodologies often used in speech or speaker recognition to the problem of PD detection or assessment, given the maturity of the techniques used in those areas. In this sense, in many other areas of speech processing, a number or studies are exploiting *Deep Learning* (DL) strategies, which allow building end-to-end systems that are capable to learn relevant features from raw data or transformations of the input data, having provided impressive results compared to other more traditional approaches [7,22]. Unfortunately, most of the methodologies dealing with the analysis of pathological speech -including PD- disregard the use of DL, mainly due to the restrictions in the size of available data sets. In Cummins et al. [11], a thorough review was made to analyse which type of artificial techniques were used in 6 editions of two popular challenges dedicated to speech analysis: the *Computational Paralinguistics Challenge* (COMPARE) and *Audio/Visual Emotion Challenge* (AVEC). During the analysed editions, the challenges addressed different problems including the detection of upper respiratory tract infections, alcohol intoxication, autism, depression, and the assessment of pathological speech, among other speech-related health problems. The authors found that, unlike speech recognition and other contexts where DL has been successfully applied, most of the approaches that provided the best results in either COMPARE or AVEC challenges were based on handcrafted -or engineered- features and more conventional artificial intelligence techniques, such as ensemble methods, and support vector machines. According to the literature review, only in two cases the winning team used some deep network architecture, despite that in most of the editions at least one of the submitted papers proposed an approach based on DL. Bearing this in mind, the authors claim that the main reason for this result is the lack of databases with a large number of samples, which are required to properly train DL models and avoid phenomena such as overfitting. This is because DL architectures have, by definition, a large number of parameters that have to be estimated, thus considerable amounts of data are required to properly compute these parameters and generate, subsequently, reliable DL models. The scarcity of large databases of pathological speech is a well-known problem in the field, which has been discussed previously in literature [17]. To deal with the insufficiency of data, Cummins et al. made some recommendations about the steps that could be taken to overcome such problems, including the exploitation of *transfer learning* techniques to combine databases with similar content, along with the use of feature learning strategies.

Transfer learning is a methodology that allows transferring part of the information harvested by models trained in different but related contexts, and where typically large amounts of data are available, to other models that intend to solve a different task, but where the available data sets are significantly less abundant. The transfer learning strategy requires a new model to be trained, but starting from the previously trained -or pre-trained model-, in such a manner than instead of tuning a large number of parameters, only a small proportion is adjusted. As a result the amount of required data decreases considerably in comparison to a conventional training procedure starting from scratch. In the context of speech, this idea has been used before in approaches like the *Universal Background Models* (UBM) [40] based on *Gaussian Mixture Models* (GMM), extensively used for speaker verification, and also pathological speech detection/evaluation tasks [14,17]. Although the potential of transfer learning to set up the use of DL in the context of pathological speech assessment has already been pointed out, not many efforts have been taken in this direction.

With this in mind, the goal of this paper is to introduce the challenges that are faced when using a DL methodology based on speech for PD detection and assessment, more particularly for the assessment based on the UPDRS scale. This work evaluates a feature engineering approach, on which characteristics often used in voice condition analysis are used to train a DNN model. Likewise, a feature learning strategy based on transfer learning -which uses a model previously trained in an automatic voice condition assessment task- is employed to transfer part of the learned information to a new model to predict a three-level UPDRS score. Instead of mel-spectrograms, which are the standard for speech recognition task, the input to the model are transformations of the input speech based on *Modulation Spectra* (MS) and estimated in a frame based approach. MS have been successfully used in different works related with the characterisation of pathological voices, but because of the large amount of data they contain, it is always necessary to extract some hand-tuned statistics [29,30] or to use feature selection techniques [26]. Based on the results published in [2] this work uses MS transformations as a base voice-representation to explore the feature learning approach in the assessment of PD. Finally, both feature engineering and feature learning methodologies are combined in a multimodal approach which evaluates the potentiality of mixing heterogeneous source of information to increase performance in the UPDRS prediction. This paper is organised as follows: Section 2 introduces the methods followed, Sect. 3 presents details of the methodology, the experimental setup and the obtained results; finally, Sect. 4 presents the discussion and conclusions of the work.

2   Methods

A prototypical automatic speech-based system is composed of two major stages (although others can also be considered): characterisation and decision-making. The first is carried out to extract features (or characteristics) that serve to describe a certain trait of interest (such as parameters that describe dysarthria in PD patients), while the latter is in charge of mapping from the features to a certain label that categorises the input speech (such as PD patients or controls). In particular for this paper, three different types of speech-based systems for PD assessment are considered, depending on the configurations followed in the characterisation and decision-making stages: feature engineering, feature learning and a multimodal approach mixing feature engineering and feature learning. Feature engineering is referred to a process of meticulously selecting parameters, that serve to describe the phenomena at hand. These characteristics can be extracted directly from the times series or from transformations of the times series in other domains. These are then used as feature vectors that serve as input to the next stages of analysis. In a feature learning approach (or representation learning) a multi-layer system is feed with the raw signal, or a transformation, intending to find the most useful characteristics for decision-making purposes automatically. The basis of the feature engineering configuration -in the context of DL- is the use of Deep Neural Networks (DNN) composed only of dense (or fully connected) layers, while the basis for the feature learning approach is the use of Convolutional Neural Networks (CNN) which are typically composed of convolutional layers that are in charge of collecting the relevant information from the input, and also dense layer to make the final decisions. Both types of networks are shown in Fig. 1 and will be introduced in the following sections. Notice that the CNN networks contains before its output a series of layers that shrink the size of the layer's outputs and encode the final decision of the model. Examples of methodologies based on feature engineering and feature learning are illustrated in Fig. 2. These will be explained in the following sections, along the more detailed configurations employed for experimentation in this paper.

2.1   Characterisation

Before the actual extraction of characteristics, a short-time analysis is carried out to divide the non-stationary speech signal into quasi-stationary segments. This procedure consists of a *framing* operation to divide the input speech into chunks and a *windowing* operation to taper the frames to improve spectral properties [16]. This procedure is often followed in speech analysis applications, including the analysis of pathological speech for the diagnosis of PD as in [32]. Each one of the frames can be then processed using a *feature engineering* or a *feature learning* approach, which will serve thereafter to train the systems based on artificial intelligence.

Feature Engineering: In particular for this paper, well-know features often used in voice pathology detection or assessment are employed in the feature

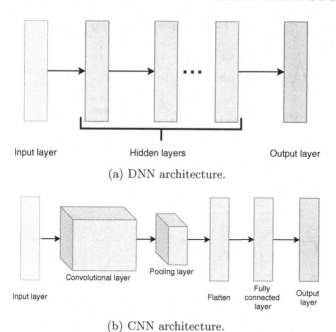

(a) DNN architecture.

(b) CNN architecture.

Fig. 1. Configurations of the DL machines considered in the paper. Figure (a) introduces a DNN approach and (b) a CNN approach.

engineering configuration. These have been grouped into sets according to the signal processing technique that is used, following the guidelines of [2,17,18]: perturbation, spectral/cepstral and complexity. For each one of the frames, the three sets of features are extracted, using Hamming windows of 40 ms for the perturbation and spectral/cepstral sets and windows of 55 ms length for the complexity set. The sets of features considered in this work are presented next:

- *Perturbation features* measure the presence of additive and modulation noise on the voice. Within this set, *Normalised Noise Entropy* (NNE) [24], *Cepstral Harmonics-to-Noise Ratio* (CHNR) [12] and *Glottal-to-Noise Excitation Ratio* (GNE) [28] are considered.
- *Spectral and cepstral features* analyse the harmonic components of the voice. These include MFCC (with no derivatives), *smoothed cepstral peak prominence* CPPS and *Low-to-High Frequency Spectral Energy Ratio* (LHr).
- *Complexity features* characterise the dynamics of the system and its structure. These include classical dynamic invariants such as the *Correlation Dimension* (D2), the *Largest Lyapunov Exponent* (LLE), and the *Recurrence Period Density Entropy* (RPDE) [25]; features which measure long-range correlations, such as *Hurst Exponent* (He) and *Detrended Fluctuation Analysis* (DFA) [25]; regularity estimators such as *Approximate Entropy* (ApEn) [38], *Sample Entropy* (SampEn) [41], *Modified Sample Entropy* (mSampEn) [45], *Gaussian Kernel Sample Entropy* (GSampEn) [46] and *Fuzzy Entropy* (FuzzyEn) [10];

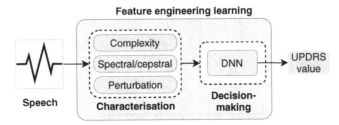

(a) Feature engineering learning with a DNN architecture.

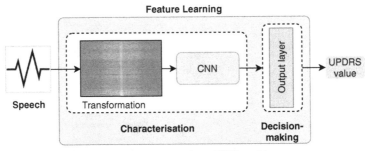

(b) Feature learning with a CNN architecture.

Fig. 2. Deep learning approaches, introducing (a) a feature engineering, and (b) feature learning architecture.

and other entropy/complexity estimators such as the *Permutation Entropy* (PE) [47], the *Lempel-Ziv Complexity* (LZC) and the Shannon (s) and Rényi (r) estimators of the *Markov Chain Entropy* (H_{MC}), *Conditional Hidden Markov Process Entropy* (H_{HMP}) and *Recurrence State Entropy* (H_{RSE}) [3,4].

The features are then utilised to feed a DNN, which is employed for the decision-making stage. A DNN is a type of neural network characterised by the presence of several hidden layers between the input and the output layer, as shown in Fig. 1a.

Feature Learning: For the purposes of this paper, a representation learning approach based on a transformation of the input speech through MS is considered. MS is employed to characterise modulation and acoustic frequencies of input voices [5], following a short-time basis using frames of 180 ms as proposed in [29,30]. After having obtained the MS representations, a CNN is used to automatically extract information from MS in the context of PD assessment. A CNN is a type of neural network characterised by the presence of several layers that process multidimensional information, such as that contained in an image, through -typically- convolutions, pooling and flattening operations. The strngth of CNNs lies in learning hierarchical layers of concept representation corresponding to different levels of abstraction. A typical CNN is shown in Fig. 1b. The convolutional layer involves processing the multidimensional information of the input layer through filtering operations. Likewise, the pooling layer acts as a sub-sampling layer that reduces the dimensionality of the previous layer. A flatten layer is in charge of converting the multidimensional information into vector form, allowing to be connected to a fully connected layer.

2.2   Classification and Decision Making

The decision-making stage is in charge of providing an output label based on the input signal that is processed (characterised either through a feature engineering or a representation learning approach), which for the current paper is related to the severity of the disorder according to the UPDRS scores. In other words, decision-making is in charge of providing a decision about the class to which the input speech belongs. In DL approaches, this stage is composed of the particular network architecture used to process the features extracted from the data, as well as the loss function used as criterion to train the network. Unlike feature engineering approaches where the DNN is designed apart from the set of features, in the feature learning approach the whole process is carried out at once; there is only one network architecture where some layers are intended to extract the relevant patterns from the data and some other layers are designed to make the final decision. Moreover, all the layers are trained with the same purpose: to minimise the loss function.

Traditionally, training *Artificial Neural Networks* (ANN) is performed from scratch using a data set created for a specific target task. Since ANN and specially DL models could easily have hundreds of thousands of parameters, the number of samples required to properly train the models is extremely large. By contrast, a transfer learning approach consists on reusing a previously and well-trained model which are fine-tuned to produce a better final model than one trained using the original data solely. Take into account that this approach could be used either in DNN or CNN models, but in this paper it will be used only in CNN and in a multimodal approach that is to be described in the following sections.

In this work, the CNN architecture is based on the *Convolutional Module* (ConvMod) proposed in [2] (see Fig. 3), which uses two parallel pipelines of convolutional layers, emulating the idea followed recently in different speech processing tasks [49], on which 1-dimensional convolutions are employed to process spectrograms. In this manner, the first pipeline performs convolutions in the acoustic axis whilst the other one performs convolutions in the modulation axis. A transfer learning strategy was used to better train the CNN. For these purposes, an auxiliary database serves to pretrain the ConvMod module. Then, this pretrained module is transferred to a new model which was fine-tuned using a database of parkinsonian voices. Figure 4 shows a schematic of the transfer learning procedure.

As in [2], the output layers of the different architectures considered in this paper vary whether the problem is assumed to be classification or an ordinal

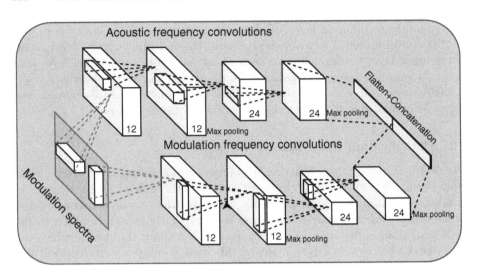

Fig. 3. Convolutional module used by the CNN architecture, following a methodology similar to the one in [2]. Image adapted from [2]

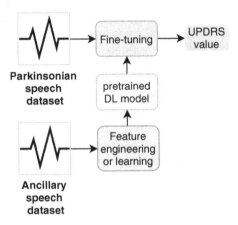

Fig. 4. Transfer learning scheme

regression, and therefore the corresponding loss functions are changed accordingly. In a pure *classification* task, the activation function of the output layers corresponds to a soft-max function. Thus, the most suitable loss function should be a standard categorical cross-entropy. However, to deal with class imbalance in the data, the loss function is replaced by a *Weighted Categorical Cross-Entropy* (*WCC*) as given by:

$$\mathcal{L}_{WCC} = -\frac{1}{N} \sum_{i=1}^{N} \sum_{j=1}^{C} \mathbf{1}_{y_i \in C_j} \omega_j \log p_{model}[\hat{y}_i \in C_j] \tag{1}$$

The term $\mathbf{1}_{y_i \in C_j}$ is the indicator function of the i-th observation (out of N) belonging to the j-th category. The $p_{model}[\hat{y}_i \in C_j]$ is the predicted probability for the i-th observation belonging to the j-th class. When there are more than two classes, the neural network outputs a vector C, where each value in the vector refers to the probability that the network input is classified as belonging to the respective category. ω_j is the weight associated to the error when the true class is j. In this work the weights ω_j, are adjusted to balance the importance of all the classes during training.

Bearing in mind that the prediction of discrete PD score according to the UPDRS scale is an *ordinal classification* problem, this works evaluates a surrogate ordinal regression function, which uses a regular soft-max activation function in conjunction with a double weighted categorical cross-entropy loss function. This function is denoted as *Ordinal Classification* (*OC*) and is as follows:

$$\mathcal{L}_{OC} = -\frac{1}{N} \sum_{i=1}^{N} \sum_{j=1}^{C} \mathbf{1}_{y_i \in C_j} \upsilon_{ij} \omega_j \log p_{model}[\hat{y}_i \in C_j] \qquad (2)$$

where $\upsilon_{ij} = 1 + |C_i - j|$ and C_i is the true class of the sample i. The first weight is the same ω_j incorporated in Eq. (1) to compensate for the imbalance problem. The second weight penalises the errors of the model in accordance to how far the predicted class is from the ground truth.

3   Experiments and Results

3.1   Corpora

Three datasets are considered in this paper: Neurovoz, GITA and the *Saarbrücken Voice Database* (SVD). Both Neurovoz and GITA are the target datasets and contain registers of PD patient and control speakers, while SVD is used for the transfer learning approach, due to its larger size in comparison to Neurovoz and GITA, i.e., SVD will serve to create a pretrained model which will be fine-tuned using the information of the PD datasets.

Saarbrücken Voice Database: SVD contains registers of more than 2000 German speakers phonating different vowels and uttering a short sentence. Registers were recorded at a sampling frequency of 50 kHz and 16 bits of resolution. For this paper purposes, the same subset of 568 normophonic and 970 pathological subjects included in [17] is used.

Neurovoz: The dataset has been recorded in collaboration with the *Ear, Nose and Throat* and *Neurology* services of the *Gregorio Marañón hospital* in Madrid, Spain. It contains registers of 47 PD and 35 control speakers whose mother tongue is Spanish Castilian. Speakers are recorded carrying out a series of speech tasks including diadochokinetik tests, the repetition of phrases, monologues or the sustained phonation of vowels. The subset utilised in the present study contains one registers of the vowels /a/, /i/ and /u/. All of the patients were under pharmacological treatment and took the medication between 2 and 5 h before the speech recording. All the patients were diagnosed and labelled according to the UPDRS and Hoehn & Yahr scales by neurologist. More details about the dataset could be found in [31,33]. PD patients and control group are balanced in age and sex.

GITA: This corpus contains a variety of speech tasks from 50 PD patients and 50 control speakers whose native language is Spanish Colombian [35]. All the patients were diagnosed and labelled according to the MDS-UPDRS and Hoehn & Yahr scales by neurologist. PD patients and control group are balanced in age and sex. Similar to NeuroVoz, speakers are recorded carrying out a series of speech tasks including diadochokinetik tests, the repetition of phrases, monologues and the sustained phonation of vowels. From all the speech tasks that were recorded, only the registers of the sustained vowels /a/, /i/ and /u/ are considered for the analysis.

3.2 Setup

Experiments are carried out following a training, validation and test split of the data. A 5-folds stratified cross-validation strategy is used to split the data into training and test sets. The training set was divided again using a 5-fold stratified cross-validation strategy into training and validation sets. The aim is to estimate the performance of the systems using a completely independent set of samples to the ones used for training and hyperparameter selection. The reported results correspond to the performance obtained in the test set. To evaluate the performance of the proposed approach, two metrics are employed: *Balanced Accuracy* (BACC) and *Average Mean Absolute Error* (AMAE). BACC is a classification measure normalised with respect to the number of samples per class, which is defined as:

$$BACC = \frac{1}{C} \sum_j \frac{1}{N_j} \sum_{\forall i \in C_j} [\![\hat{y}_i = y_i]\!] \tag{3}$$

where $[\![\cdot]\!]$ is and indicator function giving 1 if the condition is satisfied and 0 otherwise. N_j is the number of samples in the j-th class.

AMAE is a balanced measure computing the average deviation between the predicted and the true class, and which is defined as follows [6]:

$$AMAE = \frac{1}{C} \sum_j \frac{1}{N_j} \sum_{\forall i \in C_j} |\mathcal{O}[y_i] - \mathcal{O}[\hat{y}_i]| \tag{4}$$

where y_i are the true and $\hat{y}_i$ the predicted labels; and $\mathcal{O}[\cdot]$ is an operator indicating the position of the label in the ordinal rank (i.e., if a certain label y_i can take up values $0, 1, 2$ and the label is 2, its position is 3).

Three different DL architectures for the automatic assessment of voices are presented in this paper. These include a DNN architecture based on feature engineering (Fig. 1a), a CNN architecture based on representation learning (Fig. 1b), and multimodal architecture that combines both feature and representation learning. These are described in the next sections.

Feature Engineering-Based DNN Architecture: The *DNN architecture* is designed to process the set of characteristics in the feature engineering approach, therefore it consists of a conventional multi-layer perceptron with two hidden layers and one output layer. Since the speech signals are characterized following a frame-based approach, for every utterance, the set of features described in Sect. 2.1 are computed on each one of the considered frames. These are then processed using a statistical module, to extract the mean and standard deviation per speaker, in such a manner that the resulting feature vector is used as input to the DNN system. This DNN system is considered the baseline model for comparison purposes, hence, two different versions of the model are used, one for the classification of PD patients and controls, and another one for the UPDRS score prediction.

Feature Learning-Based CNN Architecture: The *CNN architecture* employed in this paper is designed to process the multidimensional representations obtained after having applied a MS to the input speech, following an approach similar to the one in Fig. 1b. However, due to the limited amount of parkinsonian speech, a transfer learning approach was considered within this architecture. As it was pointed out above, the proposed CNN is based on the ConvMod proposed in [2] (see Fig. 3), which uses two parallel pipelines of 1D convolutional layers. In this manner, the first pipeline performs convolutions in the acoustic axis whilst the other one performs convolutions in the modulation axis. Every pipeline contains 4 1D convolutional layers with the following number of filters: (12,12,24,24). The filter sizes are of (1,8) and (8,1) for acoustic and modulation frequency convolutions respectively.

The original architecture proposed in [2], used a multimodal approach where MS extracted from three different vowels were processed in parallel through ConvMods, and then the outputs were concatenated to feed the subsequent layers of the network. This was designed focusing on the automatic assessment of voice quality according to the GRB scale. The reason to use multiple inputs was because according to [1], there are evidences indicating the usefulness of including vowels /i/ and /u/, and not only /a/, for the assessment of certain traits of the GRB scale.

Unlike the architecture in [2], it was found that using different sustained vowels was not relevant for capturing different aspects of the UPDRS scale. Therefore, the proposed architecture does not include different inputs per vowel, but it uses a multi-instance approach where every vowel is processed through the same network, and the final decision about the PD score, for a given speaker, is computed using the maximal joint probability of every class for all the utterances (one per vowel). In order to use a short-time analysis of the voice signals, the proposed architecture uses a *time-distributed layer* where the ConvMod is applied to the MS of every frame. Then, a custom layer is employed to estimate the variance of the ConvMod's outputs, for all the frames This layer is intended to capture instability on the acoustic and modulation frequencies, which could be associated to tremor or other long time perturbations due to the presence of PD. The output of the variance layers is then processed by two fully connected layers aimed to make the final decision. The dense layers are composed of 32 and 3 neurons respectively. A schematic representation of the CNN architecture is presented in Fig. 5.

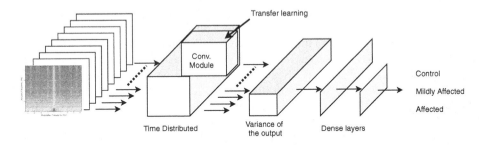

Fig. 5. Proposed feature learning-based CNN architecture using transfer learning

Since the available PD datasets contain just some dozens of speakers, and in order to reduce the number of parameters to be adjusted, a transfer learning methodology was followed and the ConvMod that was pretrained for the GRB assessment problem, is transferred to the proposed architecture. In this manner, during the fine-tuning phase, the PD voice signals were only used to train the final dense layers.

Multimodal Architecture Based on Feature and Engineering Learning:
The *multimodal architecture* is designed to combine the feature learning and feature engineering approaches, exploiting the previous knowledge obtained by the feature set described in Sect. 2.1, and the information automatically captured by the feature learning approach. In this case, the network architecture is quite similar to the former one, except that in this case, the output of the first dense layer is concatenated with the feature vector and then passed as input to two additional dense layers (see Fig. 6). The dense layers in this case contain 64, 32 and 3 neurons respectively.

All the models were trained using an Adam optimiser with a learning rate of $5e^{-3}$ and no decay rate.

3.3   Data Preprocessing

Only part III of the UPDRS scale (UPDRS-III) is considered in the analysis. The reasons are two-fold. The first is that the UPDRS-III is computed in accordance to the motor cues present in PD, and the second is the existence of an item related to the examination of speech defects due to PD.

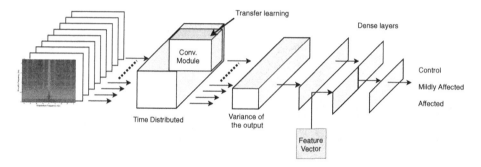

Fig. 6. Proposed Multimodal architecture that combines feature engineering and feature learning approaches

The first difficulty when designing an automatic system with the available corpora is related to the differences in labels that exist between GITA and NeuroVoz: GITA was labelled according to the MDS-UPDRS scale whilst the NeuroVoz corpus was labelled using the UPDRS scale. Supported by the results reported in [21], the UPDRS-III score values of NeuroVoz were normalised to the MDS-UPDRS-III by adding seven points to the scores of the first version of the UPDRS-III as suggested by the authors.

After this normalisation, and in order to address the assessment of PD based on the UPDRS-III scale, groups of patients were categorised according to the severity of the disorder, in such a manner that subjects presenting similarities in UPDRS-III values were grouped into some predefined categories. This procedure serves to deal with some of the imbalance that is present in the dataset, given that there are not enough samples of UPDRS-III values along the whole spectrum of the scale. The categorisation was followed using the procedure proposed in [27], where four groups are defined according to some UPDRS-III cut-off values that split conditions into: control (0), mild $(0, 32]$, moderate $(33 - 58]$ and severe (> 59). However, because of the limited number of recordings of moderate and severe patients, in both GITA and NeuroVoz, these two classes were grouped in one single class simply called *affected*. As a result, the 3-level classification of the UPDRS-III score corresponds to the following criteria:

- 0: Control
- $(0, 32]$: Mildly affected
- > 32: Affected

The distribution of the groups after the normalisation and the categorisation procedures is presented in Fig. 7. Mix is referred to the combination of both GITA and NeuroVoz datasets. The age and sex distribution per condition of GITA and Neurovoz is presented in Fig. 8.

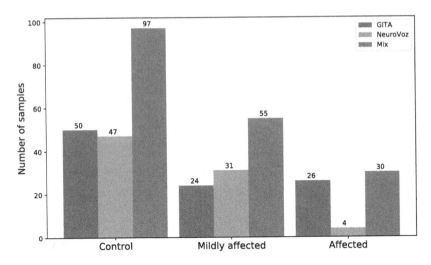

Fig. 7. Distribution of the groups in the GITA, NeuroVoz and Mix (GITA+NeuroVoz) datasets.

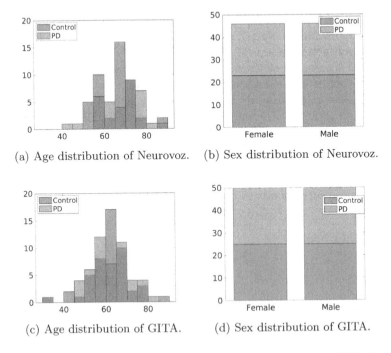

(a) Age distribution of Neurovoz.   (b) Sex distribution of Neurovoz.

(c) Age distribution of GITA.   (d) Sex distribution of GITA.

Fig. 8. Age of sex distribution per condition of the Neurovoz and GITA datasets.

3.4   Results

Table 1 shows the results obtained using the DNN architecture, in a feature engineering basis, using all the features described in Sect. 2.1. This is considered the baseline model for comparison purposes, since it is similar to the standard methods used for pathological voice assessment/detection. The performance metrics include BACC and MAE for the PD/Controls detection problem, and for the 3-level UPDRS-III score prediction problem. The results achieved by the DNN network are not the best reported results in the state of the art for PD detection using sustained vowels, but as it was pointed out before, they are intended to serve as reference points for the sake of comparison with other DL architectures. In general, the performance of the models using the GITA database is better than in the NeuroVoz database, this could be explained due to a large number of samples in the first database, but also because GITA database is more balanced with respect to the mildly affected and affected groups, whilst NeuroVoz contains only four samples in the affected group.

Table 1. Results of the DNN architecture for the PD/control and 3-level UPDRS score prediction problems

	PD/control		UPDRS score	
Corpus	BACC	AMAE	BACC	AMAE
GITA	0.70 ± 0.06	0.32 ± 0.06	0.50 ± 0.09	0.69 ± 0.17
NeuroVoz	0.65 ± 0.08	0.36 ± 0.08	0.33 ± 0.04	0.78 ± 0.10
Mix	0.68 ± 0.07	0.34 ± 0.07	0.50 ± 0.10	0.62 ± 0.09

Figure 9 presents the confusion matrix for the best result obtained using the DNN model when considering the prediction of the 3 levels of the UPDRS score. In this case the model was trained and tested using samples from both GITA and NeuroVoz datasets (Mix). According to Table 1 and Fig. 9, the performance of the system when both corpora are mixed is better in terms of AMAE for the UPDRS score prediction problem, even though the performance in the PD/control problem worsened 2% in average.

Table 2 shows the results of the feature learning-based CNN architecture, for the UPDRS score prediction problem, using the pretrained convolutional module (using transfer learning). The results are between 4% to 9% lower (depending on the dataset), in comparison to the reference model. Take into account that in this case the network implements a feature learning strategy based on MS. For the bi-class problem, this architecture achieves a $BACC$ of 0.60 ± 0.07 and an $AMAE$ of 0.42 ± 0.07 using both GITA and NeuroVoz databases, which is a performance than is similar to the observed in previous works based on feature engineering approaches, using MS as the basic representation of the voice signals [30]. In contrast, if transfer learning is not used and the entire model is trained from scratch, the performance of the systems drops down to a $BACC$ of $0.35 \pm$

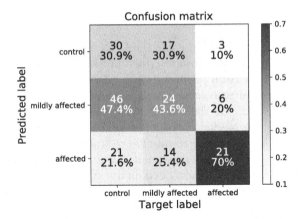

Fig. 9. Confusion matrix for the UPDRS score prediction problem using the DNN architecture and the mixture of the databases

0.03 and a $AMAE$ of 0.88 ± 0.14 using both GITA and NeuroVoz databases. In this case the model is overfitted even in the earliest iterations, and as a result the model loses the generalisation capabilities gained due to transfer learning.

Table 2. Results of the CNN architecture for the 3-level UPDRS score prediction problem using transfer learning

Corpus	BACC	AMAE
GITA	0.41 ± 0.05	0.78 ± 0.06
NeuroVoz	0.37 ± 0.04	0.88 ± 0.05
Mix	0.43 ± 0.09	0.80 ± 0.18

Table 3 shows the result of the multimodal architecture that combines the feature learning and feature engineering approaches. The most relevant result is that in this case, there is a performance improvement in comparison with the former strategies, which means that the model finds some complementary information in both approaches. Likewise, part of the information captured through the convolutional module is new and relevant for the UPDRS score prediction problem. The improvement is of about 2% of BACC in absolute terms, although in terms of MAE there is an improvement for the two databases individually. Surprisingly when the two corpora are used together, then MAE increases 2% in comparison to the DNN architecture. These results show that the size of the databases is still quite limited to provide stable results for DL models.

Finally, Fig. 10 shows the confusion matrices for the two last evaluated DL architectures for the prediction of the UPDRS score using the combination of the GITA and NeuroVoz corpora. From the figure it is possible to observe that the improvement of last architecture is mainly due to a better classification of level 2

Table 3. Results of the multimodal architecture using feature and engineering learning for the 3-level UPDRS score prediction problem.

DB	BACC	AMAE
GITA	0.52 ± 0.07	0.57 ± 0.11
NeuroVoz	0.41 ± 0.09	0.70 ± 0.12
Mix	0.52 ± 0.06	0.64 ± 0.12

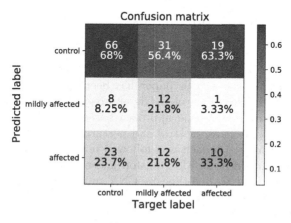

(a) CNN architecture

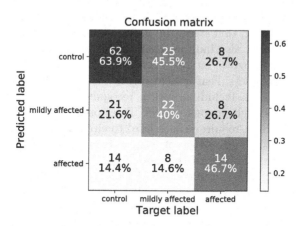

(b) Multimodal architecture

Fig. 10. Confusion matrices of the best models using: (a) feature learning and (b) the combination of feature learning and feature engineering approaches Sect. 2.2

(mildly affected). However, it is important to highlight that for all the classes, the errors committed by the multimodal architecture are more concentrated in the classes which are closer to the actual label, an expected behaviour in an ordinal classification problem. Similarly to the results reported in [2], the performance of the loss functions $\mathcal{L}_{WCC}$ and $\mathcal{L}_{O}C$ perform very similarly. The best results for the DNN and CNN models were obtained using the surrogate ordinal classification loss function, and the best results for the multimodal architecture were obtained using the weighted categorical cross-entropy.

4   Discussions and Conclusions

This paper has presented the design of an automatic system based on speech, for the prediction of UPDRS scores. Unlike other methodologies presented in the literature, the purpose of this paper has been to experiment and analyse the potentiality and limitations of a DL approach in the assessment of PD. To this end, a feature engineering approach based on DNN and three sets of features: complexity, spectral/cepstral and perturbation were considered. Likewise, a feature learning approach was followed using a CNN to automatically extract characteristics from an MS transformation of the input speech. A pre-trained model was used to fine-tune to CNN model. Finally, an architecture that combined both the feature learning and feature engineering approach in a multimodal scenario was also tested out.

Results indicate that the multimodal architecture achieved an improvement with respect to the other architectures for all the DB configurations. Likewise, feature engineering approaches are still the most appropriate in the context of PD assessment, but also that it can be used in conjunction with feature learning approaches. Results also indicate that the use of feature learning based on MS transformations provides interesting results that should be studied in more detail with larger data sets. Feature learning is becoming the standard for many speech processing tasks, including speech recognition, speech conversion, sentiment analysis in speech, among others. The potential of such a approach is undeniable, but its data requirement is hard to circumvent. In this work, it was possible to evidence the advantage of using a transfer learning strategy, which can contribute to the training of the models by the incorporation of data harvested in a different but related context. However, the currently available data sets for PD assessment are still too small for the fine-tuning phase. In other words, although larger datasets of parkinsonian speech signals are imperative for a better comprehension of the impacts that PD produces on the communication abilities of the patients, and also for the advance of the technology in this field, transfer learning has a great potential for speeding up the development of computer-aided systems that support the diagnosis/assessment of the PD patients.

It is important to highlight that, transfer learning is not novel in the context of pathological speech analysis. Indeed, the well-known GMM-UBM techniques could be considered an example of transfer learning, as the UBM model is often trained using a large data set, and fine-tuning phases are carried out to derive class-specific models (GMM-UBM) from the pretrained UBM. This strategy has been applied successfully in several works in the context of pathological speech, evidencing the recurrent data scarcity problem [14, 17, 31]. Although in the fine-tuning phase of an ANN model, typically only the last layers of the network are adjusted, the number of parameters to be modified could easily be larger than those in the case of a GMM-UBM approach, making the ANN approach clearly more data demanding. This is why transfer learning strategies should be accompanied by data augmentation strategies and larger data sets.

Given the outcomes, it can be concluded that despite some encouraging results of some of the tested architectures, the use of DL in the context of UPDRS prediction still requires further study with other, and hopefully, larger databases. Indeed, all the available datasets of PD could be considered small, with no more than 100 subjects being recorded in the best case scenario. For this reason it is probable that the whole spectrum of UPDRS values (ranging from 0-132) is not covered completely. However, for the algorithms to work correctly, it is necessary to have curated data, that is representative of the phenomena under study (such as one that covers the whole UPRS spectrum). Indeed, the larger and the more diverse this data is, the more likely a good DL model is trained. If on contrary some areas of the UPDRS spectrum are scarce or underrepresented, the generalisation capabilities of the system are at risk.

For all the above reasons, it is imperative to increase the volume of the current databases, or to record new ones that counteract these problems. Other strategies to mitigate the under-representation problem might include procedures based on *data agglomeration* (which consists of concatenating multiple sources of data such as various datasets of parkinsonian speech), or *data augmentation* to generate novel synthetic data [48]). With respect to data agglomeration, it is important to highlight that concatenating source of information that are dissimilar in terms of the population, might introduce variability that hinders the performance of the system. One example arises when considering a dataset recorded under noisy conditions, and another in a perfectly controlled environment. Unless the algorithms -or the designer- of the system properly find features that are indifferent to the recording conditions of the datasets, the performance of the system might be affected. In reference to data augmentation techniques, the objective is to generate new samples from the existing data samples -typically through transformations- that allow to artificially increase the size of the dataset. Perhaps one of the most popular data augmentation technique in the design of automatic speech analysis system are the generative adversarial networks [19], which have shown impressive performance in other speech analysis areas. Data augmentation strategies could also be accompanied by training schemes based on unsupervised learning, by using, for instance autoencoders, which allows the use of larger speech corpora -as the ones used for speech recognition- in order to obtain better initial models before any transfer learning strategy is applied.

With the respect to the transfer learning approach, the results have demonstrated the utility of the technique to increase performance when data is scarce.

However, more experimentation is foreseen, especially when including data from other contexts such as speech or speaker recognition. In particular, it would be interesting to include articulatory information, besides the phonatory information introduced by the sustained phonation of vowels, by means of transfer learning strategies using architectures and pretrained models coming from speech recognition. There exist a series of well-performing and openly available models, coming from tools like Kaldi [39], which could be explored for these purposes. The main advantage of these pretrained models is the large amount of data with which they have been trained, and which could be in the range of hundreds or thousands of hours of speech.

It is worth noting that the UPDRS scale depends on the subjective assessment made by a human evaluator, therefore it is likely that some of the provided evaluations are not correct. For this reason, certain procedures could be followed to diminish these effects. Some authors suggest, for instance, to combine the use of unsupervised and supervised algorithms to overcome the clinician-dependent labelling procedures [9]. In this manner, the information extracted by the supervised algorithms -dependent on the labels- could be supplemented by the information extracted automatically from the data and which be independent on the label. Another issue regarding the UPDRS scale is the inherent lack of correlation to the phenomena describing parkinsonian speech. Indeed, the UPDRS scale includes only one item that is directly related to analysis of speech. The remaining are mostly descriptors of the major motor cues used in clinical practice for the evaluation of PD, such as bradikinesia, rigidity, tremor, etc. Some authors have described other assessment scales that are more in concordance to the nature of parkinsonian speech, such as the Frenchay assessment scale [36] or variations [44]. Although promising results have been reported using these scales, much research is still needed as the reported works found in the literature employ a limited number of patients. Certainly, the extraction of conclusions about the usefulness of the UPDRS scale for describing parkinsonian speech, or evidences of other scales that correlates better to PD, relies on the need of having larger databases, hopefully assessed by several evaluators to reduce intra and inter variability in the scores.

Finally, an interesting approach that remains as future work is the consideration of other data transformations besides MS of the input speech. In this sense, different frequency, time-frequency or any other type of transformation might result more appropriate to characterise the phenomena relevant to PD speech (dysarthria, disprosody, dysphonia). This information, might also complement the information given by MS, permitting its processing from a feature learning perspective, even in parallel.

Acknowledgments. This work was supported by the Universidad de Antioquia, Medellín, Colombia, and the Ministry of Economy and Competitiveness of Spain under grant DPI2017-83405-R1.

References

1. Anand, S., Skowronski, M.D., Shrivastav, R., Eddins, D.A.: Perceptual and quantitative assessment of dysphonia across vowel categories. J. Voice **33**(4), 473–481 (2019)
2. Arias-Londoño, J.D., Gómez-García, J.A., Godino-Llorente, J.I.: Multimodal and multi-output deep learning architectures for the automatic assessment of voice quality using the grb scale. IEEE J. Selected Topics Signal Proces. **20**(2), 413–422 (2020)
3. Arias-Londoño, J.D., Godino-Llorente, J.I.: Entropies from markov models as complexity measures of embedded attractors. Entropy **17**(6), 3595–3620 (2015)
4. Arias-Londoño, J.D., Godino-Llorente, J.I., Sáenz-Lechón, N., Osma-Ruiz, V., Castellanos-Domínguez, G.: Automatic detection of pathological voices using complexity measures, noise parameters, and mel-cepstral coefficients. IEEE Trans. Biomed. Eng. **58**(2), 370–379 (2011)
5. Atlas, L., Shamma, S.A.: Joint acoustic and modulation frequency. EURASIP J. Adv. Signal Process. **2003**(7), 310290 (2003)
6. Baccianella, S., Esuli, A., Sebastiani, F.: Evaluation measures for ordinal regression. In: 2009 Ninth International Conference on Intelligent Systems Design and Applications, pp. 283–287. IEEE (2009)
7. Bahdanau, D., Chorowski, J., Serdyuk, D., Brakel, P., Bengio, Y.: End-to-end attention-based large vocabulary speech recognition. In: 2016 IEEE International Conference on Acoustics, Speech and Signal Processing (ICASSP), pp. 4945–4949. IEEE (2016)
8. Bhidayasiri, R., Martinez-Martin, P.: Clinical Assessments in Parkinson's Disease: Scales and Monitoring, vol. 132. Elsevier Inc., 1 edition (2017)
9. Cerasa, A.: Machine learning on Parkinson's disease? Let's translate into clinical practice. J. Neurosci. Methods **266**, 161–162 (2016)
10. Chen, W., Peng, C., Zhu, X., Wan, B., Wei, D.: SVM-based identification of pathological voices. In: Proceedings of 29th Annual International Conference of the IEEE EMBS, Lyon, France, pp. 3786–3789 (2007)
11. Cummins, N., Baird, A., Schuller, B.J.: Speech analysis for health: current state-of-the-art and the increasing impact of deep learning. Methods **151**, 41–54 (2018)
12. de Krom, G.: A cepstrum-based technique for determining a harmonics-to-noise ratio in speech signals. J. Speech Lang. Hear. Res. **36**(2), 254–266 (1993)
13. De Lau, L.M., Breteler, M.M.: Epidemiology of parkinson's disease. Lancet Neurol. **5**(6), 525–535 (2006)
14. Espinoza-Cuadros, F., Fernández-Pozo, R., Toledano, D.T., Alcázar-Ramírez, J.D., Lopez-Gonzalo, E., Hernandez-Gomez, L.A.: Reviewing the connection between speech and obstructive sleep apnea. Biomed. Eng. Online **15**(1), 20 (2016)
15. Goetz, C.G., et al.: Movement disorder society-sponsored revision of the unified parkinson's disease rating scale (mds-updrs): scale presentation and clinimetric testing results. Mov. Disord. **23**(15), 2129–2170 (2008)
16. Gómez-García, J.A., Moro-Velázquez, L., Godino-Llorente, J.I.: On the design of automatic voice condition analysis systems. part i: Review of concepts and an insight to the state of the art. Biomed. Signal Process. Control **51**, 181–199 (2019)
17. Gómez-García, J.A., Moro-Velázquez, L., Godino-Llorente, J.I.: On the design of automatic voice condition analysis systems part ii: Review of speaker recognition techniques and study on the effects of different variability factors. Biomed. Signal Process. Control **48**, 128–143 (2019)

18. Gómez-García, J.A., Moro-Velázquez, L., Mendes-Laureano, J., Castellanos-Domínguez, G., Godino-Llorente, J.I.: Emulating the perceptual capabilities of a human evaluator to map the GRB scale for the assessment of voice disorders. Eng. Appl. Artif. Intell. **82**, 236–251 (2019)
19. Goodfellow, I., et al.: Generative adversarial nets. In: Advances in Neural Information Processing Systems. pp. 2672–2680 (2014)
20. Gustavsson, A., et al.: Cost of disorders of the brain in Europe 2010. European Neuropsychopharmacology **21**(10), 718–779 (2011)
21. Hentz, J.G., Mehta, S.H., Shill, H.A., Driver-Dunckley, E., Beach, T.G., Adler, C.H.: Simplified conversion method for unified parkinson's disease rating scale motor examinations. Mov. Disord. **30**(14), 1967–1970 (2015)
22. Hinton, D., et al.: Deep neural networks for acoustic modeling in speech recognition: The shared views of four research groups. IEEE Signal Process. Mag. **29**(6), 82–97 (2012)
23. Hughes, A.J., Daniel, S.E., Ben-Shlomo, Y., Lees, A.J.: The accuracy of diagnosis of parkinsonian syndromes in a specialist movement disorder service. Brain **125**(4), 861–870 (2002)
24. Kasuya, H., Ogawa, S., Mashima, K., Ebihara, S.: Normalized noise energy as an acoustic measure to evaluate pathologic voice. J. Acoust. Soc. Am. **80**, 1329–1334 (1986)
25. Little, M.A., McSharry, P.E., Roberts, S.J., Costello, D.A., Moroz, I.M.: Exploiting nonlinear recurrence and fractal scaling properties for voice disorder detection. Biomed. Eng. Online **6**(23), (2007)
26. Markaki, M., Stylianou, Y.: Voice pathology detection and discrimination based on modulation spectral features. IEEE Trans. Audio Speech Lang. Process. **19**(7), 1938–1948 (2011)
27. Martínez-Martín, P., et al.: Parkinson's disease severity levels and mds-unified parkinson's disease rating scale. Parkinsonism Rel. Disord. **21**(1), 50–54 (2015)
28. Michaelis, D., Gramss, T., Strube, H.W.: Glottal-to-noise excitation ratio - a new measure for describing pathological voices. Acustica/Acta Acustica **83**, 700–706 (1997)
29. Moro-Velázquez, L., Gómez-García, J.A., Godino-Llorente, J.I.: Voice pathology detection using modulation spectrum-optimized metrics. Front. Bioeng. Biotechnol. **4**(1) (2016)
30. Moro-Velázquez, L., Gómez-García, J.A., Godino-Llorente, J.I., Andrade-Miranda, G.: Modulation spectra morphological parameters: a new method to assess voice pathologies according to the GRBAS scale. BioMed. Res. Int. **2015** (2015)
31. Moro-Velazquez, L., Gómez-García, J.A., Godino-Llorente, J.I., Grandas-Perez, F., Shattuck-Hufnagel, S., Yagüe-Jimenez, V., Dehak, N.: Phonetic relevance and phonemic grouping of speech in the automatic detection of parkinson's disease. Scientific Reports **9**(1), 1–16 (2019)
32. Moro-Velazquez, L., Gomez-Garcia, J.A., Godino-Llorente, J.I., Villalba, J., Orozco-Arroyave, J.R., Dehak, N.: Analysis of speaker recognition methodologies and the influence of kinetic changes to automatically detect parkinsoń disease. Appl. Soft Comput. **62**, 649–666 (2018)
33. Moro-Velazquez, L., et al.: A forced gaussians based methodology for the differential evaluation of parkinson's disease by means of speech processing. Biomed. Signal Process. Control **48**, 205–220 (2019)
34. Oktay, A.B., Kocer, A.: Differential diagnosis of parkinson and essential tremor with convolutional lstm networks. Biomed. Signal Process. Control **56**, 101683 (2020)

35. Orozco-Arroyave, J.R., Arias-Londoño, J.D., Vargas-Bonilla, J.F., Gonzalez-Rátiva, M.C., Nöth, E.: New spanish speech corpus database for the analysis of people suffering from parkinson's disease, pp. 342–347 (2014)

36. Patel, S., Parveen, S., Anand, S.: Prosodic changes in parkinson's disease. J. Acoust. Soc. Am. **140**(4), 3442–3442 (2016)

37. Pfeiffer, R.F., Wszolek, Z.K., Ebadi, M.: Parkinson's Disease. CRC Press (2013)

38. Pincus, S.M.: Approximate entropy as a measure of system complexity. Proc. Natl. Acad. Sci. **88**, 2297–2301 (1991)

39. Povey, D.: The kaldi speech recognition toolkit. In: IEEE 2011 Workshop on Automatic Speech Recognition and Understanding. IEEE Signal Processing Society (2011) IEEE Catalog No.: CFP11SRW-USB

40. Reynolds, D.A., Quatieri, T.F., Dunn, R.B.: Speaker verification using adapted gaussian mixture models. Digit. Signal Proc. **10**(1–3), 19–41 (2000)

41. Richman, J.S., Moorman, J.R.: Physiological time-series analysis using approximate entropy and sample entropy. Am. J. Physiol. Heart Circ. Physiol. **278**(6), 2039–2049 (2000)

42. Rusz, J., Cmejla, R., Ruzickova, H., Ruzicka, E.: Quantitative acoustic measurements for characterization of speech and voice disorders in early untreated parkinson's disease. J. Acoust. Soc. Am. **129**(1), 350–367 (2011)

43. Shinde, S.: Predictive markers for Parkinson's disease using deep neural nets on neuromelanin sensitive MRI. Neuroimage: Clinical **22**, 101748 (2019)

44. Vásquez-Correa, J.C., Orozco-Arroyave, J.R., Bocklet, T., Nöth, E.: Towards an automatic evaluation of the dysarthria level of patients with parkinson's disease. J. Commun. Disord. **76**, 21–36 (2018)

45. Xie, H.-B., He, W.-X., Liu, H.: Measuring time series regularity using nonlinear similarity-based sample entropy. Phys. Lett. A **372**(48), 7140–7146 (2008)

46. Xu, L.S., Wang, K.Q., Wang, L.: Gaussian kernel approximate entropy algorithm for analyzing irregularity of time series. In: Proceedings of the Fourth International Conference on Machine Learning and Cybernetics, Guangzhou, China, pp. 5605–5608 (2005)

47. Zanin, M., Zunino, L., Rosso, O.A., Papo, D.: Permutation entropy and its main biomedical and econophysics applications: a review. Entropy **14**(12), 1553–1577 (2012)

48. Zhang, Z., Cummins, N., Schuller, B.: Advanced data exploitation in speech analysis: an overview. IEEE Signal Process. Mag. **34**(4), 107–129 (2017)

49. Zhao, J., Mao, X., Chen, L.: Speech emotion recognition using deep 1D & 2D CNN LSTM networks. Biomed. Signal Process. Control **47**, 312–323 (2019)

Author Index

Arias-Londoño, Julián D.   100

Buchman, Lise Crevier   60

Choi, Jeung-Yoon   77

Dehak, N.   77
Dehak, Najim   42
Demolin, Didier   60

Gerratt, Bruce R.   1
Ghio, Alain   60
Godino-Llorente, J. I.   77

Gómez-García, J. A.   77
Gómez-García, Jorge A.   100

Kreiman, Jody   1

Moro-Velázquez, L.   77
Moro-Velazquez, Laureano   42

Ponchard, Clara   60

Shattuck-Hufnagel, S.   77

Whitfield, Jason A.   24

Printed in the United States
By Bookmasters